10 WEEK STUDY

——— *WITH VIDEO A*

THE PRESENCE CENTERED LIFE

BILL ELLIFF

THE PRESENCE CENTERED LIFE

By Bill Elliff

Published by TruthINK Publications
6600 Crystal Hill Road
North Little Rock, AR 72118

Cover Design | Dave Lewis

Editor | Tim Grissom

ISBN | 979-8-9920693-0-3

Printed in the United States ofAmerica

Dedicated to every young student who longs for more.
May they experience God's presence so deeply, just as I did in the Jesus Movement in 1970, that they will passionately pursue His nearness for the rest of their lives.

"Father, raise up a generation of Presence-centered leaders."

CONTENTS

THE WAYS OF OUR PURSUING GOD

THE WAYS OF A PRESENCE CENTERED LIFE

EVERYTHING FLOWS FROM THE PRESENCE OF THE LORD

AS YOU BEGIN ...

Most people live and die without ever becoming consciously aware of God's presence. He is all around them, like the ocean that surrounds a fish, but they are oblivious to His existence. So they flail about, desperately trying to make a life with a tragic deficiency. "Apart from Me you can do nothing,"[1] Jesus said ... and He meant it. The One who made you designed you to operate your life in His presence.

Everything flows from the presence of the Lord. Everything. If you are experiencing His nearness, you have all that you could ever need or want. Without His presence, you have nothing that matters or lasts. You were created to live in intimacy with God, consciously aware of Him all day long. The following pages are all about this awareness and the absolute necessity of close dependency upon Him.

Are you experiencing His presence? If you are, you are joyful and satisfied, peaceful and content. You have challenges, some intense, but you will never face them alone. Every day is a purposeful adventure as you walk and talk with God. Even life's darkest moments are holy and meaningful if He is with you.

But you will find yourself woefully insufficient if you do not know how to draw near to God. Or worse, you will be clueless about your inability but filled with a compensating pride that is a sad caricature of what you were created to be. You may not know how to enter into His presence or, once there, how to abide, to remain. Or, you may have experienced His presence in the past, but things have changed, and you have lost His nearness.

It is God's surprising intent to be with us. I use the word "surprising" because it is precisely that to most of us. We have believed the Big Lie about God, which we'll see in the following pages, and have settled into a life of unfruitful independence.

Don't merely read this study ... but pursue His presence. Ask God before reading each chapter to open your mind and heart. Stop at points and meditate on what God is trying to say to you. Pray these truths in. Most of all, ask God to make Himself known to you. He has gone to extraordinary lengths, even the giving of His Son, so His presence could become the foundational reality of your life.

You were made to be with Him.

Bill Elliff
Little Rock, AR
April 2025

---

[1] John 15:5

HOW TO USE THIS STUDY

Welcome to the study of *The Presence Centered Life*. God longs for us to experience His presence in deep, life-changing ways. We pray these pages and your involvement with others will take you there.

You'll notice that the study is divided into two sections.

- First, "The Ways of our Pursuing God." You will discover the great sweep of the Bible and how God has been relentlessly pursuing us. These pages will give you a whole new framework for understanding the Bible.
- Second, "The Ways of a Presence-Centered Life." This will give you a pattern for living in God's presence for the rest of your life! This is designed to give you a tool to aid you personally and to use in discipling others.

There are five daily studies and a weekly Group Discussion Guide that you will use if you are meeting with others. The group study is designed to *follow* each week's study so each participant will come in prepared.

DAILY STUDY

There's no substitute for your daily personal study. Read the opening paragraphs each day, then spend some prayerful, deliberate time answering the questions and working the truth into your heart and mind.

Don't try to see how quickly you can get through this daily time. Relax and take time. Think deeply. Meditate on the Scripture. We will use four simple tools to help us.

PLANT A SEED

Each week we will invite you to seek to memorize 1-2 Scripture verses that summarize the truth of that week. Don't let the enemy tell you that you're incapable of doing this! Ask the Holy Spirit to help you. We've devised a simple, effective way for you to review it each day.

If you want, write the scripture out on a card and place it where you will see it daily.

"Let the Word of Christ richly dwell within you," Paul said.[1] This will pay incredible dividends as you seek to develop a Presence-centered life.

DIG DEEPER

Each day there will be 4-5 questions for you to work through. Thinking through these and writing down your answers will also prepare you to discuss this better as you gather in your small group during the week.

---

[1] Colossians 3:16

■ WRAP IT UP

Ask God, "Lord, what is the one thing you're saying to me today?" and summarize it in one or two sentences. What is your takeaway for each day?

■ TALK TO HIM

A study of God's presence should *take us into God's presence!* The shortest distance to that is prayer. Spend a final few moments in deliberate communion with God. Remember: your presence with Him is His great desire!

Talk to the Father like you would to a friend. Thank Him for what He's showing you, ask Him to help you understand it and apply it in your life. Be specific in your requests to Him and see what God will do.

WEEKLY STUDY

Gather with your group weekly and walk through the Group Discussion Guide. Pray about this meeting before you come, asking God to make His presence known to all of you.

Access is included in this workbook to the group videos by Bill Elliff for the WATCH portion of your group discussion.

To access the weekly group videos, scan the QR code below or visit
billelliff.org/presencecenteredlife

Scan to watch videos

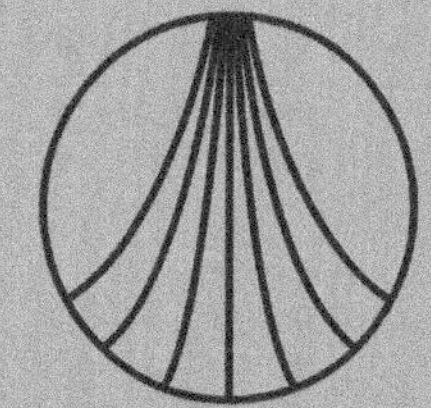

WEEK 1

THE STORY

DAY 1:

WHAT IF YOU COULD SPEND A DAY with anyone in human history? Who would you choose? Think carefully because you only have one choice.

Would it be a historical figure? Aristotle, Winston Churchill, or Abraham Lincoln? Madame Curie, Queen Elizabeth, or Harriet Tubman?

Or someone biblical? Think of spending an entire day talking to Moses, hearing about the burning bush and God's glory on Mount Sinai. Or an afternoon with the author of the Psalms, the shepherd-poet-warrior David.

Or maybe a New Testament believer? Hearing Mary Magdalene's account of her transformation and encounter with the resurrected Christ at the empty tomb. Discussing theology with Paul or spending a day with John, the disciple who leaned on Jesus' breast.

Here's the second question.

Do you think such a day would be beneficial to you? Would it change your life? Would time in their physical presence help you?

A Greater Question

But what if I told you that you could spend a whole day … *with God?*

What if you could sit at His feet for twenty-four hours? If your day would be spent in His *actual* presence discussing with Him anything you wanted … learning things that "eye has not seen and ear has not heard"?[1] What if you could understand the greatest secrets of life? What if you could ask for His power and He would give it? His wisdom and you would have it? How would your life change if He revealed to you the direction for your future?

Would this be valuable to you?

It's not only possible, but it's His deliberate intent. You were created to be with Him, but you must learn how to live in His presence. Discovering how to abide there every day is the most important thing you will ever do, for everything flows from the presence of the Lord. Everything.

The Beginning

This all begins with a story unlike any tale you've ever heard.

It is an eternal story, beginning before and lasting beyond time as we know it.

---

[1] 1 Corinthians 2:9

It is as current as today's news but predates all human history.

This tale unfolds chronologically with breathtaking intrigue. Each chapter builds upon the last, carefully designed by the Perfect Author. You cannot understand the magnitude of this story without seeing the intent of each developing chapter.

It's also a comprehensive account. It explains everything that is and ties everything in human history together. Two wonderful theologians, J. Scott Duvall and Daniel Hays, have labeled this story *God's Relational Presence: The Cohesive Center of Biblical Theology*, showing that every book in the Bible collaborates with the others to tell this story.[2]

And not just the books, but the characters too—the good and bad, the evil and righteous, the angelic and demonic, the Divine and the human—each one has been given a role in telling us what the Author wants us to know of what has been and what is to come. And right in the middle of the tale there is even found the perfect God-man, the Hero of it all. His presence is stunning.

You're in the story too! In many ways, you're what this true account is all about. When you begin to understand this overarching narrative, you will be overwhelmed by the height, depth, and breadth of God's love for you; you will be astonished by His uniquely designed purpose for your life and how beautifully you fit in it all.

The theme of the story is so expansive that it can fill every day with joy and purpose. It is so rich that you will spend eternity understanding its design.

What is this theme that will occupy your thoughts forever?

God's presence.

God desires an unbroken, daily, personal relationship with us, but we must cooperate.
His presence is our greatest need, and our presence is His great desire.

Read that again ... multiple times.

DAILY STUDY

PLANT A SEED

Read this verse 4-5 times and begin to memorize it this week, hiding it in your heart. Ask God what it means and meditate daily on it.

Psalm 16:11 | You will make known to me the path of life;
In Your presence is fullness of joy;
In Your right hand there are pleasures forever.

2 J. Scott Duvall, J. Daniel Hays, *God's Relational Presence: The Cohesive Center of Biblical Theology*, Grand Rapids, MI, Baker Academic, 2019.

■ DIG DEEPER

What do you think it means to "live in God's presence"?

"God desires an unbroken, daily, personal relationship with us, but we must cooperate." Do you think that's true? What would be different about your day if you were aware of His presence all day and interacting with Him? Be specific.

"His presence is our greatest need." In what specific ways do you need God's presence on a daily basis? List 3-5 ways.

1.

2.

3.

4.

5.

What are the typical results in your life when you don't live in God's presence for a day or more? When you are not aware of Him and communing with Him? (Examples might be an increase of worry, impatience, returning to old sins, etc.)

Is it hard for you to accept the fact that God has deliberately brought you into His story? Why is it difficult?

WRAP IT UP

Summarize what God seems to be saying to you today. What is your one-sentence takeaway?

TALK TO HIM

Spend time in prayer. Pray specifically about what you learned today.

DAY 2:
FACETIME

Roberto Garcia had an idea. It had been stimulated by his work on a video gaming platform, but Roberto took it to a whole new level. He began working with his team at Apple to perfect his idea so it could be featured on the iPhone 4, which was set to be released in 2010. It was appropriately called FaceTime® and it revolutionized communication, making it possible to not only *hear* but *see* others on a call.

Roberto said that "one of the proudest moments" in his life was initiating one of the first FaceTime calls with his mother-in-law who couldn't be present at the birth of their first child.

"We heard her bawling in crystal clear audio in the moments afterward," Garcia said. "She told me she felt like she was right there. That's what we aimed for when we created FaceTime."

The Real FaceTime

As wonderful and seemingly indispensable as FaceTime is, God has prepared us for a far more fulfilling experience, a non-stop FaceTime with Him.

The word for "face" in the Hebrew language is *panim*. It is used in the Old Testament over 2100 times. When we see the word "presence" in our Bibles, it is almost always a form of this root word. It is a word to describe intimacy, reality, nearness.

> Since that time no prophet has risen in Israel like Moses, whom the LORD knew *face to face.*[1]
>
> In your presence (*face*) is fullness of joy.[2]
>
> O God, restore us and cause Your *face* to shine upon us, and we will be saved.[3]
>
> When You said, "Seek My face," my heart said to You, "Your face, O LORD, I shall seek." [4]

---

[1] Deuteronomy 34:10, (*emphasis mine)*

[2] Psalm 16:11b

[3] Psalm 80:3, (*emphasis mine)*

[4] Psalm 27:8

"Presence" (panim) is an experiential word. If someone is present with you, they are in the room with you, in close proximity. You are "in the same place as," the dictionary says.[5] Everything is different in your relationship to someone if you are close enough to see their face.

Seeking His Face

Notice in the verses above that God invites us to "seek His face." He wants us to come into His presence. We're going to see that He doesn't just want us to visit occasionally—He wants us to abide there because His presence is our greatest need and our presence is His great desire.

DAILY STUDY

PLANT A SEED

Rehearse the verse we're learning. Fill in the blanks from memory and try to repeat it several times. Meditate on what it means.

Psalm 16:11 | You will make known to me the path of life;
In Your presence is fullness of ___________;
In Your right hand there are pleasures forever.

DIG DEEPER

Whose face brings you joy every time you see them? (List 2-3 people).

Why do their faces bring you joy? What is it about them specifically that delights or encourages you?

As you learn to enter God's presence ... what is it about God that brings you immediate joy?

What is it about Jesus that delights you? If you were standing in His presence right now, how do you think you would feel and why?

---

[5] *Oxford English Dictionary*, Oxford University Press, 2013.

Do you have a child or grandchild whose presence brings you joy? Do you think it's possible that you (as God's child) coming into His presence would bring Him great delight? That you have the possibility—just by your presence—of blessing Him? What is it about you that might delight Him right now?

WRAP IT UP

Summarize what God seems to be saying to you today. What is your one-sentence takeaway?

TALK TO HIM

Spend time in prayer. Pray specifically about what you learned today.

DAY 3:
BEING NEAR

It is one thing to know about God, but another to experience His real presence. You may say, "Well, I know that God is with me," as a fact, but are you aware of His presence? Are you abiding in His presence? Do you talk with Him?

If you know God at all, you know that you need Him. Without His presence, you have nothing that matters or lasts. But if you experience His nearness, you have everything you need.

God is present everywhere (omnipresent). But what we are describing is what we could call His near presence. Near enough to communicate with Him. Near enough to come to know Him.

God is certainly capable of making Himself known to those He has created. And indeed, He wants to be known. He has designed multiple ways to communicate with us because He knows we cannot possibly function without Him. He tells us to draw near to Him and promises that He will draw near to us.[1]

Presence, as we are describing in these pages, is the difference between knowing about someone and being their close friend, between a mere awareness and deep intimacy. Some people we only know professionally (Dr. Smith), others by deep friendship (my best friend, Gary).

If you are in the room with someone, you can talk to them—laugh and discuss things. You can shake hands or hug their neck. Your presence influences them and vice versa. But if you go away from their actual presence, that influence and relationship changes. If you don't see them for days or weeks, your relationship can even wane. Their near presence makes a difference.

For our lives to work properly, we must be near God relationally. The more we're in His presence, the better it is. God longs for this more than we can imagine because He knows that His presence is our greatest need and our presence with Him is His great desire. He made us for this intimacy. In fact, it is where this whole story is headed, for in heaven, we will see God's face forever with no interruption.

> There will no longer be any curse, and the throne of God and of the Lamb will be in it, and His bond-servants will serve Him. They will see His face, and His name will be on their foreheads. [2]

God is moving this story towards a place where we will be in His literal, physical presence, for this is where He longs for His children to be. Until then, two words from God, stated over and over in the Bible to His people, summarize this nearness: "with you."

---

[1] James 4:8

[2] Revelation 22:3–4

If we are experiencing His near presence, we have everything necessary for our lives, relationships, homes, churches, and nations. Conversely, to be separated from His presence is to lose everything that matters. The loss of His nearness explains all that is wrong with this world.

DAILY STUDY

PLANT A SEED

Walk through your verse, filling in the blanks from memory. Think of what these three phrases promise as we enjoy His nearness.

Psalm 16:11 | You will make known to me the path of life;
In Your __________ is fullness of joy;
In Your right hand there are ___________ forever.

DIG DEEPER

When you think about experiencing God's presence all day long, what word comes to mind?

- ☐ Impossible
- ☐ Scary
- ☐ Confusing
- ☐ Exciting
- ☐ Encouraging
- ☐ ___________________

How often do you think you experience a genuine awareness of God's presence?

1 2 3 4 5 6 7 8 9 10
Never | Only in crisis | Some Sundays | 2-3 times a week | Daily | Often each day

When are you most aware of God's presence? In other words, are there certain events, circumstances, or people that make you more aware of God's presence than usual?

What do you think Jesus' disciples felt each day as they were in His actual presence? Be specific.

Why do you think the disciples, after being with Jesus, were willing to leave everything and follow Him?

What is it about God's nearness that helps your willingness to follow Him fully?

WRAP IT UP

Summarize what God seems to be saying to you today. What is your one-sentence takeaway?

TALK TO HIM

Spend time in prayer. Pray specifically about what you learned today.

DAY 4:
OUR PRESENCE WITH HIM

His presence *is* our greatest need, but our presence as His great desire is hard to fathom. In fact, most of us don't believe it. Our constant enemy, Satan himself, is the vicious culprit behind our skepticism. He is the Father of Lies and has worked since the Garden to make this truth seem unrealistic. He's constantly whispering to us:

> "God doesn't care about you."
> "He doesn't want to be with you … He just wants to use you."
> "You don't really matter to Him."
> "Look at all the tragedy in this world. If God were interested in us, He would have stopped all this."
> "God just barely tolerates you. He doesn't really love you at all."
>
> … and he is relentlessly accusing us, day and night …
>
> "With what you've done, how could He allow you in His presence?"
> "Why would He be interested in someone as insignificant as you?"
> "How could you possibly have a relationship with God anyway? You're too sinful, and He's too distant."
> "He likes others way more than you. They are more significant to Him than you are."
> "What have you ever done for God?"
> "Do you realize what you just did this morning? How you failed Him? He doesn't want to be with you."
>
> … and on and on.

Have you heard these whispers?

I was with a group of 100 men on a retreat at a vibrant church, sharing some of these truths. The pastor asked if he could say something before the next session. He stood up and said to the men, "The Lord showed me something about you men while I was praying, and I want to ask you a question: How many of you feel that God just barely tolerates you at best?" Over half of the room stood to their feet. A quiet soberness fell over the room. And then there were moist eyes and some weeping. They had believed the big lie.

Do you feel that way?

If you have ever felt that God just tolerates you, then you have fallen prey to Satan's lies. He has accomplished the first step in separating you from God's nearness and cutting off your source of life and power to battle the schemes of Satan. After all, why would you seek to draw near to a God that you believed had no desire to be near you?

DAILY STUDY

PLANT A SEED

Rehearse this verse again today, filling in the blanks from memory.

Psalm 16:11 | You will make __________ to me the path of __________;
In Your presence is fullness of joy;
In Your right hand there are pleasures forever.

DIG DEEPER

Read again through the "whispers" and "accusations" that Satan uses on us. As you look through that list, put a check mark beside each one that you've heard in your heart (and believed) at times.

What words or thoughts describe how you feel God actually feels about you? (Check all that apply)

☐ Disappointed
☐ Angry
☐ Disinterested
☐ Irritated
☐ Being with you is necessary but not enjoyable
☐ Loves you but doesn't care much what you do each day
☐ Saved you and will connect with you when you get to heaven. Until then, you're on your own
☐ Occasionally concerned about you when you're in a crisis
☐ Deeply concerned about everything in your life
☐ Longs for you to walk in His presence each day
☐ He loves your presence and it delights Him when you consciously come to Him
☐ He wants you in His presence more each day

What does God gain by being with you?

What do you think Satan gains by making you think God is uninterested in your presence?

WRAP IT UP

Summarize what God seems to be saying to you today. What is your one-sentence takeaway?

TALK TO HIM

Spend time in prayer. Pray specifically about what you learned today.

DAY 5:
BELIEVING HIS LOVE

The Apostle John is referred to five times in the Scripture as the Apostle "whom Jesus loved."[1] One of the great secrets of his life and beautiful spiritual effectiveness is summed up in his first letter.

> We have come to know and have believed the love which God has for us … and there is no fear in love; but perfect love casts out fear. [2]

John was confident in how God felt about him, how perfectly Christ loved him. If you don't really know and believe "the love which God has for us," then your relationship with the Father is limited at best.[3] This has been our Enemy's plan all along, and centuries of practice have made him grievously good at his deception.

Across the Room

Remember when you were in high school (men) and saw *that girl* across the room, and your heart skipped a beat? Suddenly, she came on your radar, and you were intrigued. You asked your friend, "Do you think she'd go out with me?" and he candidly replied, "Are you kidding me? No way!"

But you persisted. "Why don't you ask *her* best friend to ask (that girl) if she would go out?" you suggested to your buddy. When that filtered through the communication chain, it got back to you that she might entertain the idea. So you asked her out and, to your amazement, discovered that she had wanted to go out with you all along! You had an awesome time on the date and asked her out again and again and again. And then, one day, you asked her to marry you, and ultimately, you had eight kids and twenty-seven grandkids! (At least, that's what happened to me!)

Imagine all you would have missed if you had not believed she wanted to be with you! Your faith in *her desire for your presence* helped you pursue and receive an incredible gift.

In His perfect love and sovereignty, God wants us to live in His presence personally, daily, and continually. He has been on an unending pursuit to bring us back into the Garden, back into His presence. In multiple, powerful ways, He is inviting us to be with Him, and it is His great delight to do so.

In the following pages and days, we will see this overarching theme through

---

[1] John 13:23; 19:26; 20:2; 21:7; 21:20

[2] 1 Jn 4:16–19

[3] 1 John 4:16

five ways that God has pursued us. In fact, you may be surprised that you didn't see this sooner, for it is the framework of the whole Bible and human history. He invites us into His presence through creation's design and voice, His calling to us, dwelling among us, indwelling us, and coming again to take us into His uninterrupted presence. But to know His daily nearness calls for a deliberate and continual response. We will see this in the second half of the book, giving us a path to enter and remain near Him without interruption through six ways that must become our pattern for living. Remember …

God desires an unbroken, daily, personal relationship with us, but we must cooperate. His presence is our greatest need, and our presence is His great desire.

The more you know the whole story, the clearer this becomes.

DAILY STUDY

PLANT A SEED

Rehearse this verse again today, filling in all the blanks from memory.

Psalm 16:11 | You will make known to me the path of life;
In Your presence is fullness of joy;
In Your __________ __________ there are pleasures forever.

Pause and thank God in prayer for what His presence promises us.

DIG DEEPER

Do you, like John, "know and believe God's love" for you? (Check one)

- ☐ Not really
- ☐ At times
- ☐ Often, but I can get confused by the enemy about how God feels about me
- ☐ By God's grace, yes, I do know it and believe it deeply!

Recall a time when you were at complete peace in knowing God loves you. What caused you to be so certain of His love?

If you struggle to accept God's love for you personally, what has caused you to doubt? Give this some careful thought. Ask the Holy Spirit to help you see what unsettles your peace and assurance.

WRAP IT UP

Summarize what God seems to be saying to you today. What is your one-sentence takeaway?

TALK TO HIM

Spend time in prayer. Pray specifically about what you learned today.

GROUP DISCUSSION

GETTING STARTED

Welcome to Week 1 of "The Presence Centered Life!" This week we began an exciting journey … and I'm glad we're doing it *together!* Hopefully, you were able to work through the daily study for the first week. Our group study is designed to follow your daily personal study each week. In this way, we will come together having already given a good bit of thought about the topic for the week. In fact, most of the questions we will ask are some you've already thought through.

What are you hoping to gain personally from this study?

What stood out to you this week?

WATCH

As you're watching the video, write any thoughts that strike you for discussion with the group afterward.

DISCUSS

Spend some time discussing. Don't feel like you have to get to every question. Let the Lord guide your conversation. Remember, you're here to help each other as you seek the Lord. Be honest and transparent.

"God desires an unbroken, daily, personal relationship with us, but we must cooperate." Do you think that's true? What would be different about your day if you were aware of His presence all day and interacting with Him? Be specific.

What is it about Jesus that delights you? If you were standing in His presence right now, how do you think you would feel and why?

Do you have a child or grandchild whose presence brings you joy? Do you think it's possible that you (as God's child) coming into His presence would bring Him great delight? That you have the possibility—just by your presence—of blessing Him? What might delight Him about you right now?

When are you most aware of God's presence?

Read again through the "whispers" and "accusations" that Satan uses on us (on Day 4). As you look through that list, which ones have you heard most often in your heart (and believed) at times.

PRAY

Spend some time praying these truths in as a group. Remember to do your daily study this week.

THE WAYS *of our* PURSUING GOD

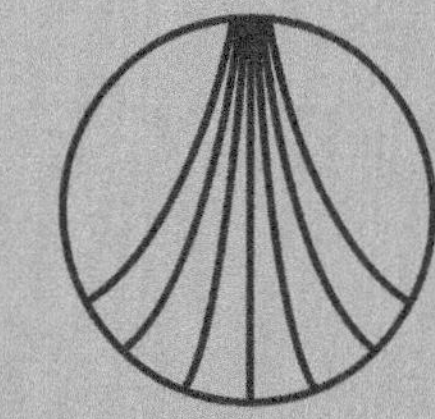

WEEK 2
CREATING

DAY 1:

IN THE BEGINNING OF TIME, the triune God—Father, Son, and Spirit—spoke the world into existence. Sun, moon, and stars appeared. Land and seas were divided. Animals, birds, and fish were designed in all their unique and breathtaking beauty. Everything needed was created and placed with Divine order. But God desired one thing more to complete His creation …

> Then God said, "Let Us make man in Our image, according to Our likeness; and let them rule over the fish of the sea and over the birds of the sky and over the cattle and over all the earth, and over every creeping thing that creeps on the earth." God created man in His own image—in the image of God He created him—male and female He created them.[1]

God was saying, "We desire more! We want to design the highest creatures with the highest purpose." The nature of God's design for this man and woman showed His plan and delight for us to be with Him, for us to enjoy an unbroken, personal relationship with Him. Our design and purpose and His presence are intricately linked. He didn't have to create us, but He made us … to be with Him.

Like Him

Unlike all the other creatures, we were made in God's image. As such, we have a soul and spirit that mirrors Him. A mind that can think, ears that hear, eyes that see, and a mouth that speaks—all so we can communicate with Him.

We were made like Him so we could live with Him and experience His presence. If we had not been made in His image, this relationship would have never occurred.

Like Him … With Personality

Because we are made in God's image, we have the characteristics of personality that He has. We too can think, reason, communicate, and create. We have emotions that feel and a will that decides. This personhood, uniquely created in us *by* God and *like* God, is placed there so we can be *with* God, so we can live joyfully in His presence.

> God is a person, and in the deep of His mighty nature He thinks, wills, enjoys, feels, loves, desires, and suffers as any other person may. In making

[1] Genesis 1:26–27

> Himself known to us He stays by the familiar pattern of personality. He communicates with us through the avenues of our minds, our wills, and our emotions. The continuous and unembarrassed interchange of love and thought between God and the soul of the redeemed man is the throbbing heart of New Testament religion.
>
> … You and I are in little (our sins excepted) what God is in large. Being made in His image we have within us the capacity to know Him. In our sins, we lack only the power. The moment the Spirit has quickened us to life in regeneration our whole being senses its kinship to God and leaps up in joyous recognition. … It is, however, not an end but an inception, for now begins the glorious pursuit, the heart's happy exploration of the infinite riches of the Godhead.[2]

Our continual presence with Him is just as essential as our eyes or ears or legs or brain. We were designed to function properly *with Him*. Our design demands His nearness. He does not merely tolerate our presence, He delights in it!

DAILY STUDY

PLANT A SEED

Read this verse several times and begin to memorize …

Genesis 1:26 | "Let Us make man in Our image, according to Our likeness; and let them rule."

DIG DEEPER

Explain in your understanding of what it means to be created in God's image.

Think through how you were made in God's image and how each part of you helps connect you with God's presence. For instance:

▶What part does your mind play in allowing you to experience His presence?

▶How does it affect you when you spend the whole week never thinking about God and what He has said in His word?

---

[2] The Pursuit of God, A.W. Tozer, Moody, Chicago, ILL., 2015.

▶What difference does it make if you intentionally read, memorize, and meditate on God's Word? If you let your mind dwell on Him?

▶You have emotions, just like God. What part have your emotions played in connecting you with someone else's presence? As you love, and feel, and hurt, are angry, etc.?

▶How do your emotions affect your worship of God? When you are moved with sorrow, or lifted with joy, for instance?

■ WRAP IT UP

Summarize what God seems to be saying to you today. What is your one-sentence takeaway?

■ TALK TO HIM

Spend time in prayer. Pray specifically about what you learned today.

DAY 2:
LIKE HIM ... WITH PURPOSE

GOD MADE US LIKE HE IS so we could join Him in what He does. In His first statement about us, God defined our purpose: "Then God said, 'Let Us make man in Our image, according to Our likeness, and let them rule.'"[3]

God is a ruler; He rules over everything that exists. When He created the earth, God desired for His image bearers to rule over this creation ... to rule just like He does, with righteousness, justice, wisdom, grace, order, authority, and love.

He wants us to rule in multiple arenas or domains. We are to oversee creation, ourselves, our families, our work, our churches, our communities, our nations.

> What is man that You take thought of him, and the son of man that You care for him? Yet You have made him a little lower than God, and You crown him with glory and majesty! You make him to rule over the works of Your hands. You have put all things under his feet.[4]

These purposes give our lives meaning. We can accomplish important things, help many people, and bring God's order and love to our part of the world. All of us long to find our purpose—we were created for this.

No human could do this alone, and so we are to "be fruitful and multiply and fill the earth."[5] Each of us is given a specific sphere in which to exercise this godly leadership. Whether we realize it or not, we have been given a realm of creation over which to rule.

But we are unable to do this properly without a personal relationship with God. Left to our own, we are sinful rulers. We cannot rule rightly if we are separated from His presence. Look at the confusion and deception, anger and bitterness, separation and loneliness, family and relational disintegration, arguments and wars that plague us. Our world has felt this tragic dissonance as we have tried to rule independently.

The very fact that we were created with this Divine purpose indicates that we were made to live in His presence. We cannot fulfill our purpose without His nearness. Again, God made us like He is, so we could join Him in what He does.

---

[3] Genesis 1:26

[4] Psalm 8:4–6

[5] Genesis 1.22

DAILY STUDY

PLANT A SEED

Read and fill in the blank:

Genesis 1:26 | "Let Us make man in Our __________, according to Our likeness; and let them rule."

DIG DEEPER

You were created by God to rule, to lead and oversee this world. What and where are the specific areas (environments/responsibilities/domains) you are to oversee?? (List all you can think of.)

Who are the people or groups of people God has placed in your life that you are to influence, help, and lead?

When you are *not* walking in God's presence, do any of the statements below characterize your leadership? (Check all that apply)

- ☐ I don't really think about my responsibilities.
- ☐ I am fairly passive.
- ☐ I make lots of mistakes.
- ☐ I tend to hurt or disappoint people.
- ☐ I get controlling.
- ☐ I do well in some areas, but ignore (or am simply unaware) of others.
- ☐ I can be selfish and not very generous.
- ☐ Other: ____

What could you do to learn where and how God wants you to lead by His desgin? Think of specific steps.

What *specific* things do you need from God to help you rule well?

WRAP IT UP

Summarize what God seems to be saying to you today. What is your one-sentence takeaway?

TALK TO HIM

Spend time in prayer. Pray specifically about what you learned today.

DAY 3:

LIKE HIM ... IN A PLACE

PLACES ARE IMPORTANT. Everything we do occurs in a place and is shaped by that environment. God created places, and He has a particular use for them.

God is omnipresent, and we are not, but He made a place for man—an exquisite Garden. This was not just a place for men and women; it was a place where God would also be. It was to be a *shared* space. He designed it so both He and our first parents had access to this place and could walk and talk there with each other. These beginning days for Adam and Eve were exactly what God desired … a perfect place shared with His perfect presence and His beautifully created beings.

Can you imagine the glory of physically walking with God in that pristine place? The immediate presence of God! Every plant and animal in its full glory! The mountains and seas, the sky above, and earth's luxurious carpet beneath. All of it untouched by sin and corruption.

If your heart is thrilled by this picture, then get ready, for there is coming something even more spectacular at the end of the story! Our Elder Brother is preparing it for us right now.

This first Garden indicated that we were made to experience God's *continual, daily* presence. The fact that God was in this Garden where He placed man indicates that He planned for us to be with Him. Why else would God design it this way if our presence with Him was not His great delight and our greatest need?

He wants to be with us!

Even man's fall could not destroy God's plan for a place with His constant presence. God has kept manifesting Himself to people in human history in thousands of places … on mountaintops and valleys, in the heavens and the seas. He met Moses in a burning bush and a needy woman at a well in Samaria. We will see His unfolding blueprint, creating many places of His presence along the way but culminating in another more glorious and eternal garden.

But think of this … He has places for you.

DAILY STUDY

PLANT A SEED

Read and fill in the blank…

Genesis 1:26 | "Let Us make man in Our image, according to Our likeness; and let them _______."

DIG DEEPER

List some of the places that have been important to you in your life thus far. Briefly describe why each one is important to you.

We don't know how long Adam and Eve lived in the Garden before their spiritual fall. Describe what you think they must have felt living in this shared space with God. Think of how you would have felt.

Where are some of the physical places where you have encountered God's presence most deeply? Was there anything unique about those places? Is there anything you did that helped create that opportunity to encounter Him so genuinely? Any common components that might be wise to understand and utilize now and in the future?

Do you have a place where you meet God every day, a place that helps you access His presence? If not, where could that be developed in your daily routine?

What did Jesus do to more deeply access the presence of His Father when He was on earth? What are ways you could do the same?

■ WRAP IT UP

Summarize what God seems to be saying to you today. What is your one-sentence takeaway?

■ TALK TO HIM

Spend time in prayer. Pray specifically about what you learned today.

DAY 4:

UNLIKE HIM ... DEPENDENT

ALTHOUGH WE WERE MADE in God's image, there is one way in which we are dramatically different from God. We are not God, and therefore we need Him. We were designed to operate in close, personal intimacy and dependency upon Him. Without His presence, we are deficient in every way.

Every man and woman mightily used by God understands this. David said, "You are my Lord. I have no good besides You."[6] Peter cried out when Jesus asked him if he was going to leave, "Lord, to whom shall we go? You have words of eternal life. We have believed and have come to know that You are the Holy One of God."[7]

Jesus taught His disciples—and all of us—this dependency through an unforgettable word picture.

> I am the vine, you are the branches; he who abides in Me and I in him, he bears much fruit, for apart from Me you can do nothing.[8]

The agnostic, C.S. Lewis, who became one of the greatest apologists of his generation, stated this clearly in his classic book, *Mere Christianity.*

> God made us: invented us as a man invents an engine. A car is made to run on petrol [gas], and it would not run properly on anything else. Now God designed the human machine to run on Himself. He Himself is the fuel our spirits were designed to burn, or the food our spirits were designed to feed on. There is no other. That is why it is just no good asking God to make us happy in our own way without bothering about religion. God cannot give us a happiness and peace apart from Himself, because it is not there.[9]

We must have His nearness—daily, hourly—to function properly. Our most significant failures come when we forget this and pridefully try to operate on our own. Remember, His presence is our greatest need, and our presence is His great desire.

---

6 Psalm 16:2

7 John 6:68–69

8 John 15:5

9 Mere Christianity, C.S. Lewis, Macmillan, New York, NY., 1980.

DAILY STUDY

PLANT A SEED

To help you memorize this verse, place your name in the blanks today and repeat it multiple times. Realize that the triune God said this one day when He created you!

Genesis 1:26 | "Let Us make (your name) in Our image, according to Our likeness; and let (your name) rule."

DIG DEEPER

Why does God allow us to wander from His presence?

What is at the root of our rebellion against God? What was it for Adam and Eve?

All of us have had seasons where we thought we could live without God. Everyone lives there before their conversion. But even after we trust Him as our Savior and His Spirit comes to live in us, we can foolishly believe we can handle life on our own. Describe the season when you were most distant from Him. What did you experience?

What brought you back to Christ?

WRAP IT UP

Summarize what God seems to be saying to you today. What is your one-sentence takeaway?

TALK TO HIM

Spend time in prayer. Pray specifically about what you learned today.

DAY 5:
SATAN'S FOUNDATIONAL ATTACK

We don't know the exact details of how Satan gained his temporary authority over the world, but we know it is real and exists under the sovereign authority and purposes of God.

But imagine the devil's terror when men and women were made in God's image. He knew the first parents would multiply and the world would be filled with beings in God's image that would threaten his rule.

But he also knew that everything depended upon these humans walking with God. They must be in His presence to function properly. And so, our adversary had one agenda: to separate us from God's presence. Through a big lie and devious temptation, he enticed Adam and Eve to doubt and disobey God, knowing that their sin would detach them—and us—from God. And he succeeded. Adam and Eve lost intimacy with God.

This will always be Satan's primary ploy. He knows that if we are separated from the presence of God, then not only will we not be ruling well and seeing God's kingdom come on earth as it is in heaven, but we will bring evil and darkness into the world, advancing Satan's evil designs. James even states that if we are friends of the world, we are enemies of God, opposing His purposes.[10]

Not only do God's creative plans indicate we were made for His presence, but Satan's attack reveals the same. We are powerful in God's presence but weak, vulnerable, and sinful without Him. We often forget this, but Satan never does.

We must realize that every attack from the enemy upon our lives is an attempt to pull us away, to distract us from the presence of God. As my friend Daniel Henderson often says, "Satan doesn't have to destroy us; he just has to distract us."

But Satan's attack in the Garden would not thwart God's desire. Our adversary won a momentary victory.

But the story was just beginning.

DAILY STUDY

PLANT A SEED

As you commit this verse to memory, see if you can find someone to share it with today and share with them what it means to you.

Genesis 1:26 | "Let Us make man in Our image, according to Our likeness; and let them rule."

---

[10] James 4:4

DIG DEEPER

Satan desperately wanted to separate Adam and Eve from the presence of God in the garden. Why? What would they lose, and what would Satan gain if this happened?

Consider how Satan tempted Adam and Eve through each of the following statements. Describe how he was "playing" them and what weakness he was exploiting.

1 Now the serpent was more crafty than any beast of the field which the Lord God had made. And he said to the woman, "Indeed, has God said, 'You shall not eat from any tree of the garden'?"
2 The woman said to the serpent, "From the fruit of the trees of the garden we may eat;
3 but from the fruit of the tree which is in the middle of the garden, God has said, 'You shall not eat from it or touch it, or you will die.' "
4 The serpent said to the woman, "You surely will not die!
5 "For God knows that in the day you eat from it your eyes will be opened, and you will be like God, knowing good and evil."
6 When the woman saw that the tree was good for food, and that it was a delight to the eyes, and that the tree was desirable to make one wise, she took from its fruit and ate; and she gave also to her husband with her, and he ate. [11]

What is Satan's ultimate agenda each time he tempts you?

What specific tactics does he use on you, pulling you away from God's nearness?

[11] Genesis 3:1–6

Satan is a "roaring lion, seeking whom he may devour,"[12] and he is out to "steal, kill, and destroy" God's sheep.[13] Understanding this, what is the greatest protection you can possibly have from Satan's devious attacks? How can you protect yourself and your family?

WRAP IT UP

Summarize what God seems to be saying to you today. What is your one-sentence takeaway?

TALK TO HIM

Spend time in prayer. Pray specifically about what you learned today.

---

[12] 1 Peter 5:8

[13] John 10:10

GROUP DISCUSSION

GETTING STARTED

I hope you had a great week of daily study in the Presence Centered Life. Remember, there are five brief daily sessions for you to work through each week before you meet with the group. Doing these faithfully will help you understand what you're studying and will also prepare you to contribute to the group.

What was your overall impression of what you learned in your study this week? Your biggest takeaway?

WATCH

As you're watching the video, write any thoughts that strike you for discussion with the group afterward.

DISCUSS

Spend some time discussing. Don't feel like you have to get to every question. Let the Lord guide your conversation.

Think through how you were made in God's image and how each part of you helps connect you with God's near presence. What part does your mind, emotions, and will play in your relationship with God?

We are created by God to rule, lead, and oversee this world. What are the specific areas (environments/responsibilities/domains) you are to oversee?

What can prevent us from ruling well? Specifically, what are things we see around us right now in our world that indicate humans are not ruling well?

Do you have a place where you meet Him every day, a place that helps you access His presence? What is it about that places that contributes to your intimacy with the Father?

All of us have had seasons where we thought we could live without God. Everyone lives there before their conversion. But even after we trust Him as our Savior and His Spirit comes to live in us, we can foolishly believe we can handle life on our own. Describe the season when you were most distant from Him. What did you experience?

We've seen this week that we must be connected to God's presence to be what we were designed to be. What are some of the ways that help you enter into God's presence and trust Him?

What is Satan's ultimate agenda each time he tempts you? What specific tactics does he use on you, pulling you away from God's nearness and what are your best tools to thwart his attacks?

Spend some time praying these truths in as a group. (Remind the group to do their daily study for the next week.)

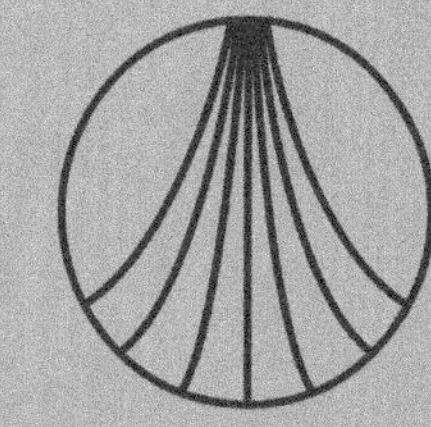

GOD CALLS US INTO HIS PRESENCE

WEEK 3

CALLING

DAY 1:
HIS CALLING VOICE

GOD COULD HAVE LEFT US in our sin and separation when we rebelled against Him in the Garden and were removed from His presence. We would have never known the glory of His nearness again. But that was not His plan. God has a glorious agenda, and He means to accomplish it.

In the next chapter of this unfolding story, we witness God's relentless pursuit as He calls us back to Himself and the garden of His presence. Each call, in each way, convinces us that His presence is our greatest need and our presence is His great desire.

Through myriad ways, He continually invites us to return to Him. He has done this through creation's voice and the call of prophets, priests, and kings. Angels are used to call us back to God's presence, as well as symbols and covenants. God encounters men and women in unforgettable places, heightening the intensity of His invitation. Most importantly, He woos us through the written Word and the Word made flesh. The only way anyone would know about God's pursuing heart is through the unending ways He calls us.

As the hymn says, "Jesus is tenderly calling [us] home."[1]

Creation

When you walk outside on a starlit night and look up, what happens to you? If you have eyes to see, you will probably think about the vastness of the heavens. *Where do they end? Who holds them in place? Who could create such unimaginable glory?*

In these moments, creation is talking to you.

The heavens are telling of the glory of God;
And the expanse is declaring the work of His hands.
Day to day pours forth speech,
And night to night reveals knowledge.
There is no speech, nor are there words;
Their voice is not heard.
Their line has gone out through all the earth,
And their utterances to the end of the world.[2]

Creation is designed to call us into God's presence. When we look up into the

---

[1] Fanny Crosby, "Jesus Is Tenderly Calling You Home," 1883.

[2] Psalm 19:1–4

limitlessness of the heavens or look down into the complexity of the DNA in a human cell, we are awestruck with Him. We realize He made everything, including us.

The more we understand how creation operates, the more we realize that it is governed by His hand and guarded by His presence. And as His creatures, we learn that we will find *our* highest purpose and joy when we are near Him. Like the rest of creation, we cannot function properly without Him. This is why the letter of James tells us, "Draw near to God, and He will draw near to you."[3]

Voices

Throughout human history, God has commissioned voices to call us to return to Him. "Choose for yourselves today whom you will serve," Joshua cried.[4] Samuel, Elijah, Elisha, Jeremiah, Isaiah—every major and minor prophet was sent by God to invite His people to come home. "Return to Me," God said through one prophet, "that I may return to you."[5] The Old Testament is the record of a relentless calling to stubborn people from a merciful Father.

But the prophets—and even the angels—were not the only voices. Believing fathers and mothers who walk with God, who have His word in their hearts, are to train their children to draw near to God.

> These words, which I am commanding you today, shall be on your heart. You shall teach them diligently to your sons and shall talk of them when you sit in your house and when you walk by the way and when you lie down and when you rise up."[6]

Wise are the parents who discover how to live in God's presence personally and then create a home where Christ is pleased to dwell. The best training would be for children to not only know *about* God but to *experience* God and learn how to live daily in His nearness.

Scripture

If these voices were not sufficient, God took extraordinary measures to write and preserve sixty-six books, His written word, the Bible. It is the God-breathed record of the history of man's waywardness and God's pursuit. It contains the literal words of God's call to us to return to Him.

We see the beautiful stories of men like David who lived with conscious awareness of God's nearness. The record of His life calls us to the Father.

---

[3] James 4:8

[4] Joshua 24: 15

[5] Zechariah 1:3

[6] Deuteronomy 6:6–7

> I have said to the Lord, "You are my Lord;
> I have no good besides You."
>
> I have set the Lord continually before me …
> You will make known to me the path of life;
> In Your presence is fullness of joy;
> In Your right hand there are pleasures forever.[7]

We read of the peace and power this brought and the tragedy of evil kings who paid no attention to God. The contrast is vivid.

Through direct commands, overwhelming promises (over 7,000 of them), and the stories of men and women who lived with or without His presence, God calls us closer to Himself on every page of Scripture.

But there is something more we must understand: the Scriptures are literally alive.

> For the word of God is living and active and sharper than any two-edged sword, and piercing as far as the division of soul and spirit, of both joints and marrow, and able to judge the thoughts and intentions of the heart. And there is no creature hidden from His sight, but all things are open and laid bare to the eyes of Him with whom we have to do.[8]

The Bible is not a stagnant history book, merely telling us how other men and women experienced the presence of God. When we read the Word, in the power of His Spirit, we encounter His living presence. Just as you are present when you speak, so God is present in His word.

We can hear Him on every page, if we have ears to hear, inviting us into His presence. We should approach the Word of God with the understanding that it is designed to lead us into direct and real communion with the Author.

DAILY STUDY

Read and begin to memorize …

Zechariah 1:3 | "Return to Me," says the Lord, "and I will return to you."

---

[7] Psalm 16:2,8,11

[8] Hebrews 4:12–13

DIG DEEPER

In times when you may have strayed from God's presence, what has He done to call you back? What circumstances, people, or scriptural truths did He use to get your attention and reassure you of His love?

What is your favorite passage of Scripture? Write it out in the space below, and then briefly describe why it is so meaningful to you.

Have you learned to turn to the Word of God to find God's direction and voice? Is His Word your final authority in all decisions? How does God's Word direct you?

Who have been some of your most helpful spiritual mentors or counselors? How has God used each one to call you to His presence?

Spend some time outside today, either walking or being still. Let the beauty and variety of God's creation move you to worship Him. Listen for Him.

■ WRAP IT UP

Summarize what God seems to be saying to you today. What is your one-sentence takeaway?

■ TALK TO HIM

Spend time in prayer. Pray specifically about what you learned today.

DAY 2:

PICTURES, PROMISES, AND PLACES

God has also given us stunning visuals that speak of Him. The Tabernacle in the wilderness (which would be more formalized later as the Temple in Jerusalem) was a powerful and lasting picture of God's presence. The progressive rooms of these sacred structures showed how sinful men must come through the sacrifice of blood to be cleansed and prepared to enter the Holy Place and the Holy of Holies ... into the very presence of God.

These symbols remind us—then and now—of how we are to live. We are to enter His presence by trusting, not in our own merits, but the sacrifice of the Lamb of God. We come through the veil that was torn, inviting us in to enjoy Him. The Temple shows us this. The continual burning of incense before the altar reminds us that we are to talk to Him morning and evening and all day in between.

These pictures were a vivid picture to the Israelites and now, through the Scriptures, they continue to remind us of where God desires us to live. His presence is our greatest need and our presence is His great desire!

Covenants and Promises

After the Garden and man's fall, we continued to run from God. But God kept calling, inviting people to join Him. He would often seal this invitation with promises and covenants. He has always had purposes for His covenant people, purposes most fully realized when we are with Him and He with us.

The summary of all God's covenants with man is profound, summed up in three realities. Every covenant, in its simplest form, said this:

1. I will be your God.
2. You will be my people.
3. I will dwell among you.[9]

The covenants and promises God made were extraordinary and undeserved. Some were dependent upon His people's obedience; others were not. Each one was a call from God to be with Him. The covenants were all designed to pull us back into His presence.

---

[9] Duvall and Hays, *God's Relational Presence*, Baker Academic, pg. 44.

Places

God also meets us in places. This began in the Garden, a place where we could be with Him and He with us.

As you scan the Bible and human history, it is remarkable to notice the places where God has chosen to meet people. God met Abraham under the heavens, using the stars as an object lesson of His faithfulness. Jacob, Abraham's grandson, would also meet God under the heavens, wrestling with Him through the night as he learned that he could not continue without God's presence.

Joseph heard God's call while in dark places: a deep well and a dismal prison, to name a few. The rejection of his own family and betrayal by close friends did not deter Joseph because he had God with him and knew that what others meant for evil, God meant for good. God's presence was sufficient.

Moses received his call at the burning bush, realizing that, although he had failed, God was not through with Him. In fact, his failing had been part of his preparation to bring him to the end of himself. The lonely wilderness ground where God trained Moses for forty years was soon to be the path of his people's deliverance. When faced with his brokenness, Moses saw God as the great I AM who would be with him in a monumental task that would move God's kingdom forward.

Later, the massive band of Hebrews that Moses was leading turned from God and worshiped a golden calf. When Moses interceded on the side of Mount Sinai, pleading for God not to leave His people, God promised, "My presence will go with you, and I will give you rest."[10]

Moses' successor, Joshua, was fearful when the task fell to him to lead the people into the Promised Land. But again, God spoke on the east side of the Jordan, assuring Him of His presence.

> "No man will be able to stand before you all the days of your life. Just as I have been with Moses, I will be with you; I will not fail you or forsake you."[11]

David encountered the Good Shepherd on the hillsides of Israel and the valley of Elah as he battled an adversary that no one else would face. He was a man after God's own heart and was uniquely used to show us the beauty of a Presence-centered life.

Daniel did not stand alone in the lion's den, nor were his friends abandoned in the fiery furnace. Stephen was in God's very presence, looking into the heavens when he was being stoned. Christ interrupted Paul on the road to Damascus and ushered him into a Presence-centered life that would change the world. Even in a dark prison cell and under the threat of persecution, Paul experienced the presence of God.

Christian history is the long story of God's presence with His people in all kinds of places. He was at the stake with John Hus as he was being burned for his

---

[10] Exodus 33:14

[11] Joshua 1:5

faith, with Corrie ten Boom in a Nazi concentration camp, with Hudson Taylor in China, and George Mueller in Bristol. The theme and glory of the ages is that God is *with us*. His presence gives us all that we need in any situation, and it is His great delight to join His children right where they are.

Scholars say that the phrase "Fear not!" is the most common command in the Bible, mentioned over 300 times. And what is the reason that a believer need not fear?

> The LORD of hosts is with us;
> The God of Jacob is our stronghold.[12]

Like a fearful child who has been picked up into the arms of his strong, sufficient father, we need not fear. We have His presence! And He has met His people in a thousand memorable places to call them back to Himself.

DAILY STUDY

PLANT A SEED

Read and fill in the blanks …

Zechariah 1:3 | "__________ to Me," says the Lord, "and I will "__________ to you."

DIG DEEPER

What specific promises has God spoken to you through His Word that led to your salvation? What happened as you trusted Him, relying on His Word?

There are 7,000 promises in the Bible! What are 3-4 of your favorite promises? How has God used them to draw you closer to Him?

[12] Psalm 46:11

What places have become sacred to you? Places where you have encountered God's presence in significant ways? What happened there?

Today's reading referred to entering the presence of God to "enjoy" Him. What does it mean to *enjoy* God? Is this true of your relationship with God? Do you enjoy Him?

WRAP IT UP

Summarize what God seems to be saying to you today. What is your one-sentence takeaway?

TALK TO HIM

Spend time in prayer. Pray specifically about what you learned today.

DAY 3:

THE SON, THE SPIRIT, AND THE BODY

We will see more about this later, but the most significant calls come directly from the lips of the Son of God who came to talk to us in person. "Come unto Me … Follow Me!" He said repeatedly. Jesus promised that after His leaving, the Father would send us His Spirit to live in you and "teach you all things, and bring to your remembrance all that I said to you."[13]

Further, the Lord established the church, which would be His body that would move through the world, calling people to come to Him. It was Christ speaking through the church that called us all to Himself through hearing the good news of what He did and would do if we would turn to Him in faith. As believers, think of how often you have been called back into fellowship with Christ because of the admonitions and encouragements, even the reproof of some loving member of the church. Even the silent witness of a humble believer, walking with God, convinces us of God's care and calls us back to Him.

> So then, we are ambassadors for Christ, as God is pleading through us. We beg you on behalf of Christ, be reconciled to God. [14]

> God is faithful, through whom you were called into fellowship with His Son, Jesus Christ our Lord.[15]

The Son, through His Spirit and His Spirit-filled body, the church, is calling us constantly into the presence of the Father. It is His unceasing invitation.

His Call to You

We have all "sinned and fall short of the glory of God." None of us deserve an invitation back into the garden of His presence. But think back over your life. How has God called you? What places, and pictures has He used? What people has He

---

[13] John 14:26

[14] 2 Corinthians 5:20

[15] 1 Corinthians 1:9

spoken through? Where have you received His promises in the night or in times of darkness or need? How has He taken His Word and Spirit and invited you home, over and over again? Think of the constancy of this call and His perseverance … and give thanks! His joy is for you to return to Him for our presence is His great desire.

Thank Him right now for His grace. And if you have never, by faith, trusted in Him as your Savior and Lord, perhaps even your reading of this today is an indication of His continued pursuit of you. He's calling now. Why would you not respond to this gracious invitation?

Softly and tenderly Jesus is calling,
Calling for you and for me;
See, on the portal He's waiting and watching,
Watching for you and for me.
Come home, come home,
Ye who are weary come home;
Earnestly, tenderly, Jesus is calling;
Calling, O sinner, come home![16]

DAILY STUDY

PLANT A SEED

Continue to commit this verse to memory …

Zechariah 1:3 | "Return to ______," says the Lord, "and I will return to _____."

DIG DEEPER

When did the Lord Jesus call you to come to Him for your salvation? What happened during that time?

[16] Will T. Thompson, "Softly and Tenderly," 1880.

The Holy Spirit lives in every true believer. He does not speak with an audible voice, but He lives in us to "guide us into all truth." He communicates with us. What are the ways and means that the Spirit uses to commune with us?

How has God used His body, the church, to call you into His presence?

Have you ever genuinely trusted Christ as your Savior? Do you know for sure that you have a personal relationship with Him? If not, perhaps now is the day to bow and humbly, gratefully ask Him to save you. The Bible makes a glorious promise for all of us:

> If you confess with your mouth Jesus as Lord, and believe in your heart that God raised Him from the dead, you will be saved; for with the heart a person believes, resulting in righteousness, and with the mouth he confesses, resulting in salvation. For the Scripture says, "WHOEVER BELIEVES IN HIM WILL NOT BE DISAPPOINTED." For there is no distinction between Jew and Greek; for the same Lord is Lord of all, abounding in riches for all who call on Him; for "WHOEVER WILL CALL ON THE NAME OF THE LORD WILL BE SAVED." [17]

If you have never done so, turn in prayer right now and call on Him to save you and give you the gift of eternal life.

If you have done that today, tell someone what has happened. Realize that God is always faithful to His promises. He will save you if you call on Him and will bring you into His presence forever!

WRAP IT UP

Summarize what God seems to be saying to you today. What is your one-sentence takeaway?

TALK TO HIM

Spend time in prayer. Pray specifically about what you learned today.

---

[17] Romans 10:9–13

GOD BROUGHT HIS PRESENCE TO US

WEEK 3
DWELLING

DAY 4:

THE DIVINE INVASION

THE GRANDEST TALES speak of warriors and kings who came to rescue others just at the critical hour. Some of these are fables; others are true accounts of selfless exploits and courageous liberations. But there is no story that rivals this one. All others are but a shadow of what C.S. Lewis called "the true myth," i.e., the greatest story in history that seems mythologic in its supernatural proportions but is actually true.

Since our fall into sin, God has gone to incredible lengths to call us to return to His presence. But only an intervention from heaven could make our return to Eden a reality.

Jesus left heaven to take the form of a man and do what was necessary to make living in God's presence possible for us. His purpose in descending to earth was to return sinful men and women, forgiven and made acceptable through His sacrifice, to God's presence. He came briefly to be with us so we could eternally be with Him. And He showed us, in flesh and blood, what being with the Father is like. Christ's *coming* was about our *returning.*

The Divine Humiliation

When God wanted to teach us what humility was in its purest form, He pointed to His Son's choice to leave heaven and take on human flesh.

> Christ Jesus, who, although He existed in the form of God, did not regard equality with God a thing to be grasped, but emptied Himself, taking the form of a bond-servant, and being made in the likeness of men. Being found in appearance as a man, He humbled Himself by becoming obedient to the point of death, even death on a cross. [1]

There could never be a more sacrificial decision than Christ choosing to inhabit the womb of a virgin girl as a one-cell organism. Facing the confines of a human body in a hostile environment, He came to dwell with us in human flesh, and we saw His presence as never before.

> And the Word became flesh, and dwelt among us, and we saw His glory, glory as of the only begotten from the Father, full of grace and truth. [2]

---

[1] Philippians 2:5-8

[2] John 1:14

This was the greatest manifestation of His presence. We could physically see Him. We could hear Him speak, watch Him respond, feel His love and grace, and observe Him under the vilest temptations of the enemy and the constant persecutions from a hostile world.

John leaned on his breast. Mary washed His feet with her hair. His mother birthed, fed, and clothed him. His adversaries taunted Him, spat on Him, and beat Him.

We watched Him with His family, closest friends, and harshest enemies. The apostle John describes the realities of His presence with us ... realities that make our joy complete!

> What was from the beginning, what we have heard, what we have seen with our eyes, what we have looked at and touched with our hands, concerning the Word of Life—and the life was manifested, and we have seen and testify and proclaim to you the eternal life, which was with the Father and was manifested to us—what we have seen and heard we proclaim to you also, so that you too may have fellowship with us; and indeed our fellowship is with the Father, and with His Son Jesus Christ. These things we write, so that our joy may be made complete. [3]

Every moment of His three decades on earth convinces us that He wants to be with us. This manifestation of His presence accomplished multiple results that could have happened no other way. If we ever doubted that God wanted to be with us, we can simply look at God in human flesh. He came because He knows that His presence is our greatest need, and our presence with Him is His great desire.

DAILY STUDY

PLANT A SEED

Read and begin to memorize ...

John 1:14 | The Word became flesh and dwelt among us and we saw His glory, glory as of the only begotten from the Father, full of grace and truth.

DIG DEEPER

Why is Christ's coming the greatest evidence that God wants us to experience His presence?

[3] 1 John 1:1-4

Think about His physical presence on earth. What do you think it would have been like to be one of His disciples, to be around Him every day?

Think of your favorite moment of Christ's life on earth. What does this moment teach you about God's presence?

Why do you think His coming in the flesh was essential for us to ultimately experience the Father's presence eternally?

■ WRAP IT UP

Summarize what God seems to be saying to you today. What is your one-sentence takeaway?

■ TALK TO HIM

Spend time in prayer. Pray specifically about what you learned today.

DAY 5:

WHAT WE SAW AND RECEIVED

Being in the presence of Christ on earth was unbelievable. And God, in His grace, recorded it through multiple eyewitnesses so we could forever see what His dwelling with us—His actual presence—was like and was for.

We saw the beauty of His Presence

What could be more attractive, what could call us to return to God more than watching Jesus in human flesh every day? He loved the outcasts. He healed the blind, the lame, and the sick. He valued women, which was uncommon in His day. He loved children with perfect tenderness. He challenged men to the noblest adventure.

He cared for those who were ignored and unseen. He even loved His enemies. He was never in a hurry but always on time. He was never fearful because His Father was speaking to Him as He moved in unceasing prayer. He was never selfish or self-seeking. In this one man who lived in perfect union with the Father, all the attributes of the perfect God-love described in 1 Corinthians 13 and the fruit of the Spirit in Galatians 5 came fully alive.

He was always at rest because He knew who He was, He knew who the Father was, and He was secure in the presence of God. He slept in a small boat through a terrifying storm. Before Pilate, he felt no need to defend Himself against false accusations. Nothing could touch Him, nothing could disturb Him, and nothing could destroy Him.

He was the ultimate model of a Presence-centered life. Perfect submission, perfect faith, perfect obedience, perfect abiding, perfect rest. He carried the optimum balance of unwavering truth and tender grace.

His beauty—the presence of God in human flesh—draws us to Him. We find ourselves loving Him because He first loved us. We want to be with Him because He first wanted to be with us.

We felt what it was like to live in His manifest Presence

God's consistent invitation is to draw near to Him and He will draw near to us. Yet, we wonder if this is possible, and if so, what it would be like. Is it best to pursue His presence? To draw near? To do what is necessary to live a Presence-centered life?

As we observe Jesus in human flesh, we see that nothing could be more beneficial, nothing more valuable. What could be better than talking to the One who has perfect wisdom? Who had it better than Peter, James, John, Mary, Martha, Mary

Magdalene, and others who were *with* Him—the One who was always righteous, always kind, always holy?

The disciples in Jesus' day were lifted to the greatest heights of living, purpose, and adventure, which they would never have experienced without being near Him. Jesus showed us that *in His presence* is the best place to be. And what was available to them is now made available to us also ... His nearness!

We became the recipients of His grace

And then, in the perfect time and way, we watched Him surrender to the hands of His enemies and go to the cross in our place. There, the Father placed the sins of the world upon Him, so one perfect Man could pay the penalty of sin for the many. He pleaded with the Father to find another way if possible but still surrendered fully to the Father's will. On the cross, His sacrifice satisfied the just demands of a righteous God for our transgressions. He paid the penalty so we would be spared.

This payment would have never been paid, of course, unless He had come to dwell with us as a man.

This ultimate humiliation and sacrifice flowed from His heart and the Father's for one purpose: that we could be with Him eternally. It was not a plot to fill a storyline or an act to make God look extraordinary (He was already all of that). It was the needed step to bring us back into His presence. And the resurrection of Christ sealed the reality. It meant that we could be in the presence of the Father and the Living Son.

God's presence is our greatest need. All our loss, sin, and darkness have come from our separation from His presence. And all our gain, righteousness, and light come when we return to His presence, made possible through Christ's life, death, and resurrection.

Christ's incarnation should convince us that our presence with Him is God's great desire. His Son was willing to come and take us there.

We beheld the Father

After the resurrection, a confused disciple said, "Lord, show us the Father, and it is enough for us," to which Jesus replied, "He who has seen Me has seen the Father."[4] If you still have doubts about the character of the Father, the reality of His pursuit of us, and the value of pursuing Him, just look at Jesus. If you live in God's presence, that is what you will experience, and God Himself will ultimately conform you to the image of His Son, the image He planned for you from the beginning.

Jesus' physical presence brought to us something that couldn't be accomplished any other way. But amazingly, there was another chapter that would follow His earthly life—another extension of the Father's pursuit as He invited us to be with Him.

---

[4] John 14:8-9

DAILY STUDY

PLANT A SEED

Read and begin to memorize.

John 1:14 | The Word became ________ and dwelt among us and we saw His glory, glory as of the only begotten from the Father, full of grace and truth.

DIG DEEPER

When you look at how the Bible describes Christ's time on earth, do you think it's possible to know His presence now in (not physical) but very real ways? Why or why not?

What does it mean that you are now a "recipient of His grace?" What has His grace brought to you that you could not have experienced otherwise?

In light of Christ's humbling act to come and live, die, and rise again on our behalf, how should we now live?

WRAP IT UP

Summarize what God seems to be saying to you today. What is your one-sentence takeaway?

TALK TO HIM

Spend time in prayer. Pray specifically about what you learned today.

GROUP DISCUSSION

GETTING STARTED

This week, we studied two of the ways of God in pursuing us: His calling of us and dwelling with us. I hope you were able to work through the daily study. It will not only help you discover what God is teaching us but also will be a reminder to enter into His presence each day … and that's our goal. We're seeking not to merely have a mind-change, but a life-change. Wouldn't it be great if we learned how to really live a Presence-centered life by the time we're through?

What did you learn overall from these two "ways" of God we studied this week?

Are you beginning to see more and more how much the Father loves you and how deeply and comprehensively He is pursuing you as He invites you into His presence?

WATCH

As you're watching the video, write any thoughts that strike you for discussion with the group afterward.

DISCUSS

Don't feel like you have to get to every question. Let the Lord guide your conversation.

God is always calling us into His presence (whether we're listening or not). In times when you may have strayed from God's presence, what has He done to call you back? What circumstances, people, or scriptural truths did He use to get your attention and reassure you of His love? (Be as honest and specific as you can).

There are 7,000 promises in the Bible! What are 1-2 of your favorite promises? How has God used them to bring you back to Him, to make you aware of His nearness?

This week's reading referred to entering the presence of God to "enjoy" Him. What does it mean to *enjoy* God? What could we do to enjoy God more every day? (The Bible says that "in Your presence is fullness of joy" (Psalm 16:11)

Why is Christ's coming the greatest evidence that God wants us to experience His presence?

Think about His physical presence on earth. What do you think it would have been like to be one of His disciples, to be around Him every day?

Does Christ desire for us to know the same things the disciples experienced? How could that be possible in our daily lives?

PRAY

Spend some time praying these truths in as a group. (Remind the group to do their daily study for the next week.)

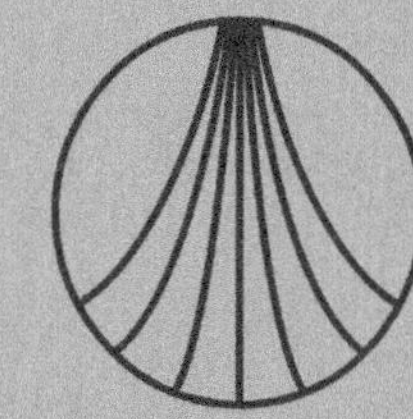

GOD INHABITS US WITH HIS PRESENCE

WEEK 4

INDWELLING

DAY 1:
THE SPIRIT

THEY WERE AFRAID. Jesus continually told His disciples that He was about to leave. This made no sense to them, for they thought He was establishing an earthly kingdom. Although the cross had been prophesied, they could not understand its purpose. And practically, they thought everything hinged on Jesus' physical presence with them.

How could they survive without His flesh and blood presence? The truths they were learning, the glory they were observing, the ministry they were experiencing, and the sheer joy of living with Jesus would be lost without Him.

The Next Step

The unfolding story of the presence of God included a chapter which the disciples could not imagine, but one that was essential for life in God's presence to be fully accomplished. Although they would not understand it until Pentecost, (How could they?) Jesus foreshadowed what was about to happen in His words before His death, recorded in John 14.

> "Truly, truly, I say to you, he who believes in Me, the works that I do, he will do also; and greater works than these he will do; because I go to the Father. Whatever you ask in My name, that will I do, so that the Father may be glorified in the Son."[1]

How could the disciples possibly do greater works than their Master? Their works would not be greater in significance but in scope. Instead of Christ being confined to one body in one place at one time, He would fill *every believer* with His presence. The Spirit of Christ, clothed in the human flesh of millions of believers, could be all over the world at the same time!

> "I will ask the Father, and He will give you another Helper, that He may be with you forever; that is the Spirit of truth, whom the world cannot receive, because it does not see Him or know Him, but you know Him because He abides with you and *will be in you.* ... In that day you will know that I am in My Father, *and you in Me, and I in you.* ... Jesus answered and said to him, "If anyone loves Me, he will keep My word; and My Father will love him, and We will come to him and *make Our abode with him.*" [2]

---

[1] John 14:12-13

[2] John 14:16-17, 20, 23 *(emphasis mine)*

Following Jesus' death, burial, resurrection, and ascension, God would send the Holy Spirit (Himself in spirit form) at Pentecost to begin a new age—an age in which every believer would be indwelt by the Holy Spirit. The Spirit of Christ would now be present all the time in each believer, giving them everything they needed to experience the uninterrupted presence of God. Just as the Father, in His endless pursuit of us, sent His Son in physical presence, now He sent His Spirit with *indwelling* presence.

In the Old Covenant, the Spirit of God came upon men and women, enduing them with power for service for a season or a task. This is why David would cry out in Psalm 51: "Do not cast me away from Your presence, and do not take Your Holy Spirit from me."[3]

To lose the Spirit upon one's life in the Old Testament age was to lose the presence of God, which was the worst fate possible, for everything flows from His presence. But in the New Covenant, following Pentecost, the Spirit would be given to every believer at the moment of their salvation. The physical presence of Jesus was no longer necessary, for His presence would now be in every true believer in the person of the Holy Spirit.

DAILY STUDY

PLANT A SEED

Read and begin to memorize …

John 14:16-17 | I will ask the Father, and He will give you another Helper, that He may be with you forever … He abides with you and will be in you."

DIG DEEPER

Why do you think the disciples were so afraid when Jesus said He was going to die?

Jesus told His disciples that they would do "greater works" than He did. What do you think this meant to them?

[3] Psalm 51:11

Do you believe that we can now do greater works than Christ? If so, how?

We've seen that "God's presence is our greatest need, and our presence is His great desire." How does the Spirit's entrance into our lives affect our ability to experience the presence of God all day long?

Read Galatians 5:22-23. This is the fruit that comes out of the life of a believer who is following the Spirit. Which of these are your greatest needs right now?

WRAP IT UP

Summarize what God seems to be saying to you today. What is your one-sentence takeaway?

TALK TO HIM

Spend time in prayer. Pray specifically about what you learned today.

DAY 2:

FULLY GOD

The Spirit of God is not a sub-level member of the Trinity; when we receive the Spirit, we have all of God we will ever have. Growth in our walk with Christ then, is learning how to be filled with the Spirit and follow His initiation … how to walk by His leadership, how to listen and follow His Spirit's prompting and the illumination of His Word.

It is also possible to quench or grieve the Spirit. Although He does not leave us, we can hinder His activity in and through our lives. We must learn more and more how to let Him have control. The question is not "How much of the Spirit do you have?" but "How much of you does the Spirit have?" We will see this clearly in the following chapters.

His presence is our greatest need, and our presence is God's great desire. This is nowhere more evident than God's willingness to literally inhabit us. God went to extraordinary lengths to send His Son to inhabit a virgin's womb for man's salvation. But think of Pentecost on equal terms. On that day, God once again humbled Himself to inhabit *every believer* by His Spirit.

Why would He take such a humbling step? So that we might be with Him and He with us. So He might fully restore us to His original purpose and plan … to see us in His own image, ruling and reigning in His power with Him and joining Him in His work.

What could be a more convincing proof that the Father desires our presence? He has come to live in us!

There is one final movement in this story … the most glorious chapter of all.

DAILY STUDY

PLANT A SEED

Read and memorize …

John 14:16-17 | I will ask the Father, and He will give you another ___________, that He may be with you forever … He abides with you and will be in you."

DIG DEEPER

What has been your understanding about who the Holy Spirit is and what He does?

In this present age, where does the Spirit dwell … and why?

Since the Holy Spirit now lives in you if you are a believer, what difference should this make?

In what ways is the Spirit working in and through your life presently?

What would happen in your family or your church if all the believers were fully controlled by the Holy Spirit who lives within them? Is this even possible?

WRAP IT UP

Summarize what God seems to be saying to you today. What is your one-sentence takeaway?

TALK TO HIM

Spend time in prayer. Pray specifically about what you learned today.

GOD IS PREPARING A PLACE FOR US IN HIS UNINTERRUPTED PRESENCE

WEEK 4

COMING!

DAY 3:
PREPARING A PLACE

I HAVE A FRIEND who has been mightily used by God. His name is known in many circles. He has a profound reputation, and his life has yielded significant, enduring fruit. If I mentioned his name, you might easily recognize it.

By the grace of God, our lives intersected years ago. I was humbled just to meet him. But as I came to know him, I was astounded to realize one day that he genuinely wanted to be with me. Before long, we were sharing beyond an acquaintance level. We enjoyed each other's company greatly. We shared common interests and passions. We laughed easily together, and we prayed fervently together. Like Jonathan and David, our hearts were "knit together in love."

I was humbled (and deeply blessed) to realize that, although separated by miles, the rest of our lives would be marked by this friendship. By God's goodness, we've been able to join together in some extraordinary ministry initiatives. For as my friend often says, "History is transformed among friends."

As astounding as that incredible realization was, there is another reality that is beyond comprehension. Christ wants to be with us! He wants to be our deepest friend. Everything from the dawn of history until the end of this age and beyond illustrates this fact. We don't believe it or even recognize its incalculable value, which is why we are often halfhearted in seeking the Lord. But it is true.

Though we've seen only the "tip of the iceberg" of this massive truth, we are awed by God's relentless pursuit of us. In ever-increasing ways, He invites us to experience His presence. He calls us, He sent His Son in human flesh to us and for us, and then He gave His Spirit to indwell us. What gifts! What glorious confirmations of His love! His presence is now constantly available to all who will join Him!

But there is one more level that exceeds all of this.

The Final Chapter

In some of His last words to His disciples, Jesus spoke of this coming intimacy we would enjoy.

> "In My Father's house are many dwelling places; if it were not so, I would have told you; for I go to prepare a place for you. If I go and prepare a place for you, I will come again and receive you to Myself, that where I am, there you may be also."[1]

[1] John 14:2-3

Jesus indicated that His ascension back to His Father was not an escape from this world. The cross, resurrection, and ascension would finish the work here that required His physical presence. Now, He was going to get something ready for us. His next assignment was to do some additional, very deliberate work and perhaps His most creative. He was going to prepare a new heaven and new earth and our eternal home.

DAILY STUDY

PLANT A SEED

Read and begin to memorize

John 14:2-3 | I go to prepare a place for you. If I go and prepare a place for you, I will come again and receive you to myself that where I am, there you may be also!

DIG DEEPER

Think of these progressive steps the Father has taken to be with us:

- ▶ He created us to be with Him and to be able to commune with Him.
- ▶ When we wandered and rebelled, He continually called us back to Himself.
- ▶ He sent His Son in human flesh to be with us and die for us.
- ▶ He sent His Spirit to indwell forever all those who would believe.

As Jesus was leaving, what did He promise that would become the final proof that He wanted us to be in His presence?

What does John 14:2-3 teach us about what Christ is doing now and what difference it will make for us in the future?

Think about a world in which we are always in the presence of God. List everything that you can imagine heaven will be like.

What should we be doing until He returns? (See Matthew 28:18-20.)

WRAP IT UP

Summarize what God seems to be saying to you today. What is your one-sentence takeaway?

TALK TO HIM

Spend time in prayer. Pray specifically about what you learned today.

DAY 4:

THE NEW GARDEN

IN THIS ETERNAL PLACE, we will enjoy His presence with no intermission. It will be a garden of absolute perfection with no hint of evil. Read John's Revelation, chapters 21-22, for just a taste of what we will enjoy. It is Eden restored, but better.

There will be no tempter and no possibility of spiritual failure. None of our relationships will be touched by evil. This is why Jonathan Edwards could write *Heaven, a World of Love* .[2] Think of living in a place where everyone loves you perfectly, you love everyone perfectly, you love God perfectly, and God loves you perfectly. (He always has, but you will understand and experience that fully.)

There was a reason why the original Garden was never meant to be our final residence. In that Garden, the Enemy had access. But in the new world, he is banished forever. Also, in our original home, we had a will with which we could choose to obey or disobey. The Spirit did not reside in us then. In the new world, we will be completely and fully redeemed, and all possibilities of spiritual rebellion will be over. There will be no distractions there. Nothing that woos us away or pulls us back into evil pursuits or mundane living. We will bask in a completely sinless environment!

And there is something else. We will live forever with the full knowledge of what we've been saved from and who did the saving. This will create an eternity of unceasing praise and rapturous joy. We will not live with the innocence of the first Eden but eternally humbled by the full knowledge of our sin and rebellion and His extraordinary pursuit of us: By Christ's grace, He came and died and rose again to deliver us from our sins, and by the Spirit's indwelling, He gave us the power to know Him on earth with intimacy and power.

This is the ultimate destination of the story … the place of His *uninterrupted* presence where we will see His face.

> There will no longer be any curse; and the throne of God and of the Lamb will be in it, and His bond-servants will serve Him; *they will see His face*, and His name will be on their foreheads.[3]

It will be life as God designed, and we will fully experience the purpose for which He made us. We will see that we were created like He is so we can join Him in what He does. And we will rule with Him, doing the precise things that each of us was uniquely created to do, with joy and perfect effectiveness forever.

---

[2] Jonathan Edwards, *Heaven, A World of Love*, Banner of Truth Trust, Carlisle, PA., 1969

[3] Revelation 22:3–4 (*emphasis mine)*

> In the flow of Revelation, at the end of Chapter 20, everything seems to have been accomplished ... Why the need for Chapters 21-22? Because the goal of salvation is not merely God's deliverance of His people from Satan and sin, but also His deliverance of His people to *Himself.* Again, the goal of the gospel is not simply salvation or deliverance from evil, but also eternal communion with God ... the final vision of Revelation spells out the primary goal and theme not only of the Apocalypse but also of the whole of Scripture: God's relational presence among His people in the new creation.[4]

Our hearts will burst with unending gratitude and our lips with unending praise for His manifest presence !

And You

Think of what we've seen in this broad sweep of God's love story. As we understand more and more of this incredible narrative, Satan's lies are fully exposed. God is not withholding from us. He loves us with an everlasting love. Like John, we can now say that "we have come to know and have believed the love which God has for us," and that "[God's] perfect love casts out fear."[5]

Let the glory of this truth wash over you like a cascading waterfall. We never again need to wonder if we are loved, accepted, desired, and useful to the Father. Our presence with Him is His great desire, and His relentless pursuit of us has proved it!

Our Father hasn't planned for a mere momentary acquaintance or something useful only to Himself. He has provided everything to bring us into an eternally growing relationship of unsurpassed meaning and boundless joy.

Remember the foundational theme of God's story? God desires to have an unbroken, daily, personal relationship with us, but we must cooperate. His presence is our greatest need, and our presence is His great desire. One day soon, this will be fully and gloriously accomplished for eternity!

DAILY STUDY

PLANT A SEED

Read and memorize.

John 14:2-3 | I go to prepare a place for you. If I go and prepare a place for you, I will come again and receive you to __________ that where I am, there you may be also!

---

[4] Duvall and Hays, *God's Relational Presence*

[5] 1 John 4:16,18

DIG DEEPER

Why is Christ's coming and taking us to heaven a glorious evidence that God wants us to experience His presence?

What would be different about a world that has no evil and no influence of Satan and his armies? What all would be gone if Satan were gone?

According to your understanding, in what ways will heaven be like the Garden of Eden? In what ways will it be different—or better?

How does the preparation of heaven for God's children indicate His love for us? How does it convince us that His great desire is our presence with Him?

WRAP IT UP

Summarize what God seems to be saying to you today. What is your one-sentence takeaway?

TALK TO HIM

Spend time in prayer. Pray specifically about what you learned today.

DAY 5:
WHAT'S NEXT?

IF OUR PRESENCE IS God's great desire, why are most believers not experiencing Him continually? Is it conceivable to experience His nearness all the time? Is the command to "pray without ceasing" even a possibility?[6] Is there more? Something we're missing?

Remember the foundational truth of the story:

God desires an unbroken, daily, personal relationship with us,
but we must cooperate.

So how do we cooperate? What is necessary?

The uniqueness we notice in a mature believer is the nearness of God. We recognize God's fragrance when we are around them. We feel His love, wisdom, and life pouring through these consecrated followers. The Father's presence with them is more constant than with others. No one is perfect, and learning how to live a Presence-centered life happens over time, but there are reasons for this abiding experience.

A Presence-centered man or woman has embraced the God-given ***means***
to consciously enter and remain in His presence.
Over time, these have become their ***ways*** *and are the keys to God's presence and power.*

The most effective among us are those who have learned how to cooperate with God continually in some non-negotiable ways—the ways of a Presence-centered life. We may be familiar with each of these components independently, but it is the union of the whole, of all of them together, that is essential. The continual practice and application of each part help us abide in His presence.

Our desire in the following pages is to put this in a way that is simple, understandable, and replicable. Memorize these six ways and use them to continually evaluate if you are experiencing His presence and, if not, to discern where you have been distracted and how to return.

We pray it will be a helpful understanding for you and a tool to help those you are discipling as you seek to live a Presence-centered life.

---

[6] 1 Thessalonians 5:17

DAILY STUDY

PLANT A SEED

Seek to share this verse with someone else this week. Share with them why this is so meaningful to you.

John 14:2-3 | I go to prepare a place for you. If I go and prepare a place for you, I will come again and receive you to myself that where I am, there you may be also!

DIG DEEPER

We have looked at five ways that God has continually showed us He loves us and wants us in His presence. Which one of these spoke most strongly to you the last few weeks and why?

▶ Creating
▶ Calling
▶ Dwelling
▶ Indwelling
▶ Coming

Can you see the common theme that runs through each of these ways? Why has God done these things in these ways toward us? What is He seeking to accomplish?

God wants us to enjoy His presence, but notice, we must cooperate. Learning to consciously live in His presence throughout each day does not just automatically happen. Over the next six weeks, we're going to look at six biblical, essential ways we must learn to cooperate with Him. If you were to guess (without looking ahead) what do you think some of those ways might be?

1. ______________________________

2. ______________________________

3. ______________________________

4. ______________________________

5. ______________________________

6. ______________________________

WRAP IT UP

Summarize what God seems to be saying to you today. What is your one-sentence takeaway?

TALK TO HIM

Spend time in prayer. Pray specifically about what you learned today.

GROUP DISCUSSION

GETTING STARTED

Have you begun to see that this theme—God's presence—is the great theme of the Bible and human history . . . that since the Garden, God has been pursuing us to bring us back into His presence?

How does this make you feel?

Read 1 John 4:16, 18 below aloud. How do these verses apply to how we should feel the more we know the ways in which God has pursued us?

> We have come to know and have believed the love which God has for us. There is no fear in love. Perfect love casts out fear.

WATCH

As you're watching the video, write any thoughts that strike you for discussion with the group afterward.

DISCUSS

Don't feel like you have to get to every question. Let the Lord guide your conversation.

Jesus told His disciples before He left that they would do "greater works" than He did. How is that possible?

We've seen that "God's presence is our greatest need, and our presence is His great desire." How does the Spirit's entrance into our lives affect our ability to experience the presence of God all day long? What has now changed for a believer?

Many people don't think about the Holy Spirit or, if they do, see Him merely as an influence. How has your understanding changed this week about the personality of the Holy Spirit (*i.e.,* who He is)?

What does His indwelling presence tell you about God's desire to be with you?

Read John 14:1-3 together. What does it teach us about what Christ is doing now and what difference it will make for us in the future?

Think about a world in which we are always in the near presence of God. List everything that you can imagine heaven will be like.

PRAY

Spend some time praying these truths in as a group. (Remind the group to do their daily study for the next week.)

THE WAYS *of a* PRESENCE CENTERED LIFE

WEEK 5

DRAW NEAR

DAY 1:

DISTANT AND DISCONNECTED

I FELT DISTANT from Christ. I had experienced this many times before, even as a pastor. This is common for most believers. But over the years, the Lord had shown me how to return to intimacy with Him. The Word of God, prayer, and fasting have always been important tools in returning; and so, in January 2010, I determined to seek the Lord in an extended fast. My one request to the Lord was that He would help me fall in love with Jesus all over again.

Toward the end of the fast, I was rewarded with an unusual sense of His nearness. It was a time of deep cleansing and renewal. I could hear His voice clearly again through His Word, and the joy of God returned to my soul. Our staff noticed this also, and many of them observed similar times of fasting and prayer and experienced the same renewal.

That fall, we felt led to call our whole church to a forty-day season of fasting and prayer. There came a deep sense of anticipation, and we began a new First Monday time of prayer, specifically praying for revival in our church, city, and nation. People would ask me about our church during that time and my standard answer was, "It feels like there is gasoline on the floor just waiting for a match." God gave us a heightened belief that He was about to manifest Himself in increasing measures.

In April 2011, I was preaching from 1 Thessalonians 5 on the quenching of the Holy Spirit. The passage says: "Do not quench the Spirit; do not despise prophetic utterances. But examine everything carefully; hold fast to that which is good; abstain from every form of evil."[1]

There is a wide range of interpretations of what a "prophetic utterance" is, but at the very least, it is when God is speaking. Paul is saying, *When God says something to you, don't ignore it or treat it lightly. Examine it carefully to make sure it is from Him and then obey.* I illustrated this that morning with this fictional—but true-to-life—thought.

> Suppose I was preparing a message from one of Paul's letters on praying for the lost. The Lord burdened me deeply through the week as I studied, and I sensed that He really wanted to say something to our people. Then imagine that, as I got up to preach, there was an unusual unction on the message. The room was quiet, the people were leaning in, and all of us knew that God was calling us to a new level of intercession for those who were far from God.
>
> As people left, they were sober and humbled and said, "Pastor, the Lord really spoke to me this morning." And then imagine that they

[1] 1 Thessalonians 5:19-22

got in their cars, went home, and *didn't make one single adjustment in their lives to pray for lost people!*

How would we describe that? God was speaking to His body, trying to mobilize them for a sacred purpose, but we had quenched the Spirit by treating His call lightly and not joining Him in what He desired to do. Think of what this response, this quenching, would do, what we would miss and how it would grieve the Lord.

As I finished that illustration, I sensed that my sermon was over, although I had many pages of notes left. I argued with God for a moment, but finally said, "I think that's all I'm supposed to say this morning."

Suddenly a retired missionary stood up in our congregation and began to cry out, "We must obey God right now!" With tears in his eyes he exhorted the people to instantly obey and not quench the Spirit. A spontaneous exhortation like that was not normal in our church.

People began to stream to the altar and they continued and continued. I walked to the floor microphone and told them to do whatever the Lord was telling them, but most of all, to not quench the Spirit. They continued to come. People were being saved, confessing their sins, going across the room to clear their consciences with others. Much was happening.

An older woman approached me and asked if she could share something publicly. As I stood beside her, she shared a sweet word. Then another came and another until there was a line. The service continued for hours until we finally concluded at 3:30 p.m.

We had a scheduled prayer gathering Monday night, and I told the people to come back and, above all else, until then, don't quench the Spirit!

The next night the building was packed. That service lasted more than three hours. It was orderly and beautiful, and God did amazing things. People were saved and baptized, money was given, folks were prayed for and gloriously delivered from many things. We knew we couldn't stop, so we invited the people to return the next night and the next.

That movement of God's Spirit lasted five weeks, every night except Saturday, in one of the most extraordinary seasons of revival I've ever known. People came from around the country to be a part of it. Most of the pastors in our city came at times and some saw fresh movements in their own churches, which was one of our most fervent prayers. We received several calls from other countries.

Our watchword was "Don't quench the Spirit." Whatever He told us to do we instantly obeyed.

Only heaven could record all that happened in those days, but here was the most glorious result: we were in the manifest presence of God with no intermission. The gospel was being spread, and lives were being changed every day. As Andrew Murray's book title suggests, we were experiencing *The Secret of His Abiding Presence.* Life became very simple—an easy yoke—for it all centered around doing nothing to lose the awareness of His presence and prompt, loving obedience to Him. It was heavenly.

These life-changing days made us all realize that a Presence-centered life is possible if we will cooperate with God. When those five weeks of spontaneous, continuous meetings ended, we did not maintain the same intensity, but we have never been the same as individuals and as a church. We learned truths about His presence and *in* His presence that we will never forget.

By the grace of God, we were learning how to draw near.

DAILY STUDY

PLANT A SEED

Read and begin to memorize …

James 4:8 | Draw near to Me and I will draw near to you.

DIG DEEPER

What was it about Bill's experience and the church's that led to the nearness of Christ? What contributed to this season?

Think of 2-3 times where you sensed the presence of Christ more deeply than any other season. How did you draw near?

Do you think God's nearness is only reserved for special times? Why or why not?

Have you ever fasted? What was difficult about it? What were the rewards?

Did you find it interesting to read that, in a time of revival, "life became very simple"? Why do you think that was the case?

WRAP IT UP

Summarize what God seems to be saying to you today. What is your one-sentence takeaway?

TALK TO HIM

Spend time in prayer. Pray specifically about what you learned today.

DAY 2:
THE NEED TO DRAW NEAR

Jesus' visit to his dear friends in the village of Bethany one day illustrates why we need to continually, consciously draw near to Him.

Christ was in the home of Mary, Martha, and Lazarus. Martha was distracted with all of her preparations. The word *distracted* literally means "drawn away." Jesus quickly realized what was happening and gave a commentary that describes all of us. When Martha grew impatient and ordered Jesus to enlist Mary to help, the Lord answered her with a kind, but strong reproof: "Martha, Martha, you are worried and bothered about so many things, but only one thing is necessary."[2]

The Son of God was standing in her house and yet Martha was angry, frustrated, and demanding. These are the normal behaviors of the spiritually diverted.

The reason we need to draw near to Christ is because we are so often drawn away. We are unaware of His presence and are living self-centered lives. The world, the flesh, and the devil bring a constant barrage of things that vie for our attention, that pull us from Him.

It is easy to wake up and realize that, although Christ is with us, we are unaware of Him, not talking to Him, and not including Him in our lives and decisions. The Word of God has become academic. Prayer is anemic. Our lives look just like Martha's. A distracted Christian doesn't look much different than an unbeliever.

> A thousand distractions would woo us away from God, but if we are wise we will sternly put them from us and make room for the King and take time to entertain Him. Some things may be neglected with but little loss to the spiritual life, but to neglect communion with God is to hurt ourselves where we cannot afford it.[3]

Stop and evaluate your life. Over the last week, how often were you conscious of the Lord's presence? Communing with Him deeply and getting your instructions in His presence? Hearing from Him personally through His Word?

Another way to evaluate is in the negative. Have you been worried, bothered, or angry? Are you frustrated at everything and nothing? Are you bored with life? Do you feel lonely, even in a crowd? Are you constantly looking for something to entertain you, to make you content and happy? Have your decisions been humanistic and not God-initiated? Is sin attractive to you, so attractive that you cannot seem to shake its grip? Is the Word of God vibrant and alive to you or merely perfunctory and dutiful? Are you living a prayerless life?

---

[2] Luke 10:41–42

[3] A. W. Tozer, *The Root of the Righteous,* Christian Publications, New York NY, 1955

DAILY STUDY

PLANT A SEED

Memorize the following verse this week. Fill in the blanks each day.

James 4:8 | Draw near to _____ and I will draw near to _____.

DIG DEEPER

How often do you find yourself distracted from the pursuit of God's nearness?

- ☐ 1-2 days a week
- ☐ 3-5 days
- ☐ Most weeks … often whole weeks at a time
- ☐ I can't remember the last time I felt very near to Christ

When you are *not* walking in God's presence, what are the clear indicators in your life? (These are important to identify. Imagine them as "check engine" lights on a car. Check all that apply.)

- ☐ My mind is centered on the things of the world
- ☐ I am worried and bothered about many things
- ☐ I'm easily irritated and angry
- ☐ I say inappropriate things
- ☐ I fall into some habitual sins
- ☐ I don't think much about Christ
- ☐ I rarely think about living my life each day to advance the kingdom of God and invest in people
- ☐ I begin to forsake my time with God in the Word and prayer
- ☐ Other: ____

What are the 2-3 things that most easily distract you, drawing you away from the Lord's presence?

What might help you to not be distracted so easily? What could you do to remain aware of God's presence and abide in Him?

WRAP IT UP

Summarize what God seems to be saying to you today. What is your one-sentence takeaway?

TALK TO HIM

Spend time in prayer. Pray specifically about what you learned today.

DAY 3:
A HUNGER AND A CHOICE

We can learn a valuable lesson from Mary's response, which is the point of this story. Unlike Martha, Mary was so hungry for communion with Christ that other demands did not pull her away. She made a deliberate choice to be "seated at the Lord's feet, listening to His word."[4] She drew near.

Lest we think that this is just the choice in the mornings during our devotions, we must remember that every moment of the common day should be filled with these choices. There's not a moment, decision, or conversation that doesn't need the power of His presence. God has given us the opportunity and the means to draw near, but we must make the choice to turn to Him. We will often be distracted, so we must often draw near. We should do it so often that it becomes habitual, that it is our "way."

Brother Lawrence, who served as a "lay brother" in a French monastery in the seventeenth century, developed a continual awareness of God's nearness. He said, "By getting up after every fall, and by frequently renewing my faith and love, I have arrived at a state of mind where it is more difficult for me not to think of God as it was at the beginning to think of Him."[5] When asked, he wrote this admonition to his friend:

> Please remember that I have recommended that you meditate often on God, day and night, during business and recreation. He is always near you and with you; do not leave Him alone. You would consider it rude to ignore a friend who came to visit you. Then why neglect God? Do not forget Him. Meditate on Him often. Adore Him continually. Live and die with Him. This is the glorious vocation of a Christian. You could say that this is our profession. If we do not know how to do it, then we must learn.[6]

We make choices all day long about what to think about, watch, and give our attention to. These were not originally natural but were learned and practiced over time until they became habitual. They are our current ways.

We pursue what we value. If we value the presence of God, we can learn to turn our minds constantly to Him, to draw near in prayer and meditation on His Word. It may take a while to wean ourselves from worldly distractions, and it can only be done by God's grace and with His help. Also, others may not understand and might think we are a bit fanatical in the fervency of our pursuit of God. But then, they may not enjoy His nearness. With practice, we can learn to draw near all day long.

---

[4] Luke 10:39

[5] Brother Lawrence, *Practicing the Presence of God*, Whitaker House, 1982.

[6] Ibid.

Practically, we can draw near by pausing throughout the day and evaluating where we are. Have we become distracted? Are we near Him or distant? What is the source of the sin and the distance we're feeling from Him?

If we have drifted, we should pause in prayer immediately and take whatever time is necessary to enter into His presence through prayer. (We will see how to draw near in prayer in the next chapter.)

DAILY STUDY

PLANT A SEED

Read and begin to memorize …

James 4:8 | _______ near to Me and I will ________ near to you.

DIG DEEPER

We do what we think is valuable. For instance, if we think television, social media, or entertainment is valuable, we'll gladly give hours to it. Why do you think Mary gave herself to "sitting at the Lord's feet" and listening to His Word? Why was this so important to her?

How important is it to you to become consciously aware of God's presence all day … and be communing with Him?

1	2	3	4	5	6	7	8	9	10
Not that important			Somewhat			Very		Most important	

What is your response to the quote by Brother Lawrence above? Do you think it's possible to be aware of God's presence all day long? Why or why not?

What would "drawing near" look like to you?

What is one significant adjustment you could make this week that would help you begin to draw near to God throughout the day?

WRAP IT UP

Summarize what God seems to be saying to you today. What is your one-sentence takeaway?

TALK TO HIM

Spend time in prayer. Pray specifically about what you learned today.

DAY 4:

THE GOOD AND LASTING PART

Jesus reminded Martha of what a Presence-centered life yields when He said, "Mary has chosen the good part, which shall not be taken away from her."[7] There is a lasting reward for those who resist distractions and turn continually to Him.

What if we made it the primary focus of each day to consciously and continually draw near to God, and then we let everything else flow from His presence? Think of what a day, a week, a lifetime in the presence of Christ would yield. One thing is certain: if we draw near to Him, He will draw near to us.

> Each of the disciples was as close to Jesus as he chose to be, for the Son of God had no favorites. With him, there is no caprice or favoritism. Their relationship with Him was the result of their own choice, conscious or unconscious. It is sobering to realize that we too are as close to Christ as we really choose to be.
>
> It would seem that admission to the inner circle of deepening intimacy with God is the outcome of deep desire. Only those who count such intimacy a prize worth sacrificing anything else for are likely to attain it. If other intimacies are more desirable to us, we will not gain entry to that circle.
>
> The place on Jesus' breast is still vacant and open to any who are willing to pay the price of deepening intimacy. We are now and will be in the future only as intimate with God as we really choose to be.[8]

DAILY STUDY

Read and begin to memorize ...

James 4:8 | Draw near to Me and I will ____________ ____________ _____ ______.

[7] Luke 10:42

[8] J. Oswald Sanders, *Enjoying Intimacy with God*, Discovery House, 2001.

DIG DEEPER

What do you think these words from Christ indicate about what Mary was doing?

> But the Lord answered and said to her, "Martha, Martha, you are worried and bothered about so many things; but only one thing is necessary, for Mary has chosen the good part, which shall not be taken away from her." [9]

Evaluate the use of your time over the past two weeks. Outside of sleeping, eating, and work, what did you give your discretionary time to? Be specific.

1.

2.

3.

4.

5.

Is there anything missing in that list that needs to be there?

What is present in that list that doesn't need to be there?

---

[9] Luke 10:41–42

Do you think it's possible to know God's presence even as you're working, recreating, interacting with others, etc.? If so, how?

WRAP IT UP

Summarize what God seems to be saying to you today. What is your one-sentence takeaway?

TALK TO HIM

Spend time in prayer. Pray specifically about what you learned today.

DAY 5:
ENTERING IN

So how do we practically draw near? The rest of this book will describe the components of drawing near to His presence and how to remain in His presence. But first, we must enter in, and the simpliest step is Presence-centered prayer.

Aren't all times of prayer Presence-centered? Not necessarily. Prayer can become routine and perfunctory, and it's possible to go through a time of prayer completely unaware of God's presence.

> Much of so-called prayer, both public and private, is not unto God. In order that prayer be really unto God, there must be a definite and conscious approach to God when we pray. In much of our prayer, there is little thought of God. Our mind is taken up with the thought of what we need and is not occupied with the thought of the mighty and loving Father from whom we are seeking these gifts.
>
> If then, we would pray aright, the first thing that we should do is to see … that we really get into His very presence. Before a word of petition is offered, we should have the definite and vivid consciousness that we are talking to God and should believe that He is listening to our petition and is going to grant the thing that we ask of Him. This is only possible by the Holy Spirit's power, so we should look to the Holy Spirit to really lead us into the presence of God and should not be hasty in words until he has actually brought us there.[10]

When Christ taught us to pray in the Sermon on the Mount, He spoke sixty words about what to say in God's presence ("Our Father who is in heaven …"). But amazingly, He gave us 120 words about *how* to enter God's presence, beginning with the words "When you pray."[11] At the heart of this explanation is a beautiful picture designed to help us know how to enter His presence … how to draw near.

> " But you, when you pray, go into your inner room, close your door and pray to your Father who is in secret, and your Father who sees what is done in secret will reward you."[12]

The great pastor, Martyn Lloyd-Jones said that when he began to understand and practice this verse, he discovered he could pray by himself or lead prayer in a crowd of thousands and enjoy deep intimacy in God's presence.

---

[10] R.A. Torrey, *How to Pray*, Moody, Chicago, IL, 2007.

[11] Matthew 6:5-10

[12] Matthew 6.6

Look at the picture Jesus gives us. See a door before you as a doorway into the foyer of heaven. Enter through the door and then turn around and shut the door. Why is this necessary? The world, flesh, and devil will throw everything at you to distract you, to pull you away from the presence of God. So shut the door on yesterday, on tomorrow, on everything that would pull you away from the throne room.

Realize you are about to have a conversation with the Father, Son, and Spirit. Then, consciously, look at the throne and worship the Father. What do you see as you look at Him? Meditate on Him in thanksgiving and praise.

What do you notice as you look at the Son, seated at His right hand? Think of all He has done for you and give thanks. And then realize that God's Spirit is present there also. We rarely speak of Him, but realize the role the Spirit plays in your life—convicting, teaching, helping, comforting. Spend time worshiping Him.

If Satan tries to accuse you and tell you that you cannot enter into God's presence, remind him of Paul's beautiful words.

> Therefore, having been justified by faith, we have peace with [literally, *facing*] God through our Lord Jesus Christ, through whom also we have obtained our introduction by faith into this grace in which we stand; and we exult in hope of the glory of God. [13]

Jesus has given us an introduction. We come trusting in Him and what He's done, and we now stand in grace. Christ provided the way for us to be here, and the Father wants us here. We are allowed to enter, not because of our good works, but His.

Utilize this image, given by Christ, to practically enter His presence, to draw near. By faith we know that He will fulfill His agreement, for He promised that if we would draw near to Him, He would draw near to us.[14]

During a particular moment in Israel's history, they recognized this value and made these choices. Wouldn't it be beautiful if this were God's testimony of our lives?

> "Yet they seek Me day by day and delight to know My ways … They ask Me for just decisions. They delight in the nearness of God."[15]

DAILY STUDY

PLANT A SEED

Recite this verse that you've now memorized. Ask God in prayer to give you an opportunity to share it with someone today and tell them what it now means to you.

James 4:8 | Draw near to Me and I will draw near to you.

---

[13] Romans 5:1–2

[14] James 4:8

[15] Isaiah 58:2

DIG DEEPER

Today is an exercise of prayer … of drawing near.

Do exactly what you just read about.

- Imagine a door.
- Open the door and step into the throne room of heaven.
- Realize Christ has given you an introduction into this "grace in which you now stand." You stand before the throne of God and have peace as you face Him, for your sins have been forgiven through Christ.
- What do you see as you look at the Father? Spend time giving Him thanks for everything you see. Praise Him for who He is and what He's done.
- Look to the right hand of the Father and notice the Lord Jesus seated there. Spend time giving Him thanks for the many things He has done for you.
- The Holy Spirit is present with you also. Think of what He has done for you as He has come to live in you—teaching, guiding, correcting, comforting. Thank Him for all these things.
- Ask the Father, "Lord, is there anything you want to say to me right now?" and then be still before Him and listen.

Spend a few moments reading Psalm 16, a psalm about the heritage we have in His presence. Thank God for everything that you see in that psalm that God has given you.

- Linger in His presence. Worship Him with a song if one comes to your mind.
- Now ask Him to make you aware of His presence all day long. Ask Him to make you aware of distractions that would pull you away throughout the day.
- Leave this prayer time open-ended and seek to talk with Him throughout the day about everything that concerns you.

WRAP IT UP

Summarize what God seems to be saying to you today. What is your one-sentence takeaway?

TALK TO HIM

Spend time in prayer. Pray specifically about what you learned today.

GROUP DISCUSSION

GETTING STARTED

We spent the first four weeks studying the overall definition of the presence of God and the overview of God's ways in pursuing us. Remember our key thought:

God desires an unbroken, daily, personal relationship with us, but we must cooperate. His presence is our greatest need, but our presence is His great desire.

We are now studying ways to enter His presence daily and to remain there … to abide. We call this diagram (that we see at the beginning of each chapter) the "Abiding Wheel" for it is to be a continual tool to help you remember the most important components to abide in a Presence-centered life. Memorize these six "ways" of a Presence-centered life and let them master you in the days ahead.

The first way of entering in and experiencing God's presence is to "Draw Near." What do you think this means?

WATCH

As you're watching the video, write any thoughts that strike you for discussion with the group afterward.

DISCUSS

Don't feel like you have to get to every question. Let the Lord guide your conversation.

Share about a time when you sensed God's nearness deeply. What contributed to that? What brought you there? What were the results?

The reason we need to consciously draw near every day (and throughout the day) is because we are so easily distracted. What are the things that regularly distract you?

Who has the most to gain by distracting you? What do you lose, and what does God lose when you are pulled away and not aware of His presence?

We do what we think is valuable. For instance, if we think television or social media is valuable, we'll gladly give hours to it. Why do you think Mary gave herself to "sitting at the Lord's feet" and listening to His Word? Why was this so important to her?

Read out loud and respond to the quote by Brother Lawrence on Day 3. Do you think it's possible to be aware of God's presence all day long? Why or why not?

PRAY

Spend some time praying these truths in as a group. (Remind the group to do their daily study for the next week.)

WEEK 6

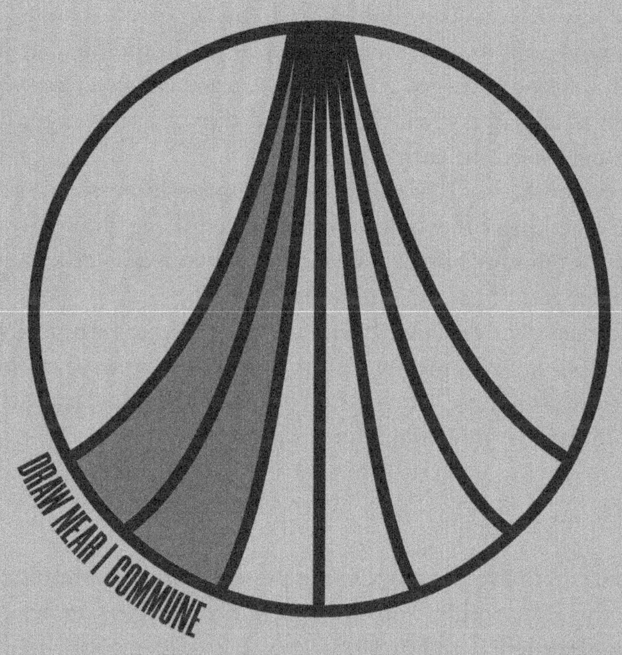

COMMUNE

DAY 1:

TALKING WITH THE FATHER

WHAT IF YOU NEEDED to take a ten-hour road trip? You then discovered that someone in your church needed to go the same city, and the two of you decided to travel together, although you really didn't know each other.

On the day of your trip, they picked you up at your home, but for some reason, you did not speak to each other when you got in the car. The silence seemed a little awkward, but you shrugged it off. *Maybe they're just not a morning person*, you thought. But ten hours later, when they stopped the car and you got out, neither of you had said a single word the entire time!

Now, besides the fact that this would be almost impossible, and the strangest trip in history, something else would have happened. Even though you sat two feet from each other for ten long hours, you would not know each other any better at the end of the trip than you did at the beginning.

Why? Because conversation is the capital of a relationship. If you don't talk, you will not come to know someone, and they will not know you. But suppose you had talked non-stop for those ten hours. You would be highly acquainted friends. Maybe even good friends. You would know each other.

With the Father

God has designed you to live and move in His presence, and communication with Him is the means of this relationship. You can't truthfully say that you have a relationship with God if you never talk with Him.

He has given you all the necessary tools to build this communion, and two are non-negotiable: His Word and prayer.

DAILY STUDY

Read and begin to memorize …

Colossians 3:16 | Let the word of Christ richly dwell within you.

DIG DEEPER

Many followers of Christ have never learned how to commune with God through the Word and prayer. They don't know that it is not optional to those who want to know His presence. It is the path to His presence each day.

Would you say that you are better at ...

- ☐ reading the Bible or
- ☐ praying?

How would you describe your communication with God? (Check all that apply).

Through His Word ...

- ☐ I read the Bible sporadically.
- ☐ I read the Bible about once a week.
- ☐ I read the Bible most days.
- ☐ I read the Bible, but ...
  - ☐ Honestly, it's fairly boring to me.
  - ☐ I don't feel like I'm communing with God, just reading a book.
  - ☐ I have trouble understanding the Bible.
  - ☐ It doesn't seem personal to me.
  - ☐ Often, I feel like I'm actually hearing from God (not audibly, but genuinely).
  - ☐ I can't wait to get to my Bible most days. It's a joy to commune with Him.
  - ☐ I come to the Bible with anticipation that God is going to speak to me.
- ☐ I memorize and meditate on the Bible at times.

Through prayer ...

- ☐ I'm not happy about this, but I find I can go many days without even thinking about praying.
- ☐ I don't really know how to connect with God in prayer.
- ☐ Prayer is boring to me. I say the same things over and over again.
- ☐ I wonder if prayer works or makes any difference.
- ☐ I try to pray, but I don't feel I'm talking with God.
- ☐ I pray when I get in a crisis or have a real need.
- ☐ I find myself praying almost every day.
- ☐ I look forward to a dedicated time each day to meet with God in prayer.
- ☐ I am learning more and more how to pray about everything.
- ☐ Prayer is as natural as breathing to me.

If you could have what you desire, what do you wish your communing with God would look like in a normal week? (Be specific).

What would be some steps of action you could take to have that kind of communion with Him daily?

WRAP IT UP

Summarize what God seems to be saying to you today. What is your one-sentence takeaway?

TALK TO HIM

Spend time in prayer. Pray specifically about what you learned today.

DAY 2:

COMMUNING THROUGH THE LIVING WORD

If there is a dominant theme in the Bible, it is God's constant admonition to read, study, and meditate on His Word. This is to be more than mundane reading, though. It involves letting God talk to you and letting His Word take up residence in you.

The apostle Paul said you must "let the Word of Christ richly dwell within you."[1] To "dwell" means to settle down, to be at home. God has given us sixty-six books of His God-breathed words, and He desires for His words to find a deep, permanent home in our hearts. He knows that enjoying His presence depends upon our constant and rich conversations with Him.

> All Scripture is inspired [God-exhaled] by God and profitable for teaching, for reproof, for correction, for training in righteousness; so that the man of God may be adequate, equipped for every good work. [2]

If you will listen to Him daily through His Word: "It shows you the path to walk on; that's doctrine. It shows you where you got off the path; that's reproof. It shows you how to get back on the path; that's correction. And it shows you how to stay on the path; that's instruction in righteousness." [3] He knows what is necessary to perfectly equip you for everything He wants you to do, but you must talk to Him and let Him talk to you. Continual study and meditation on His Word are the means.

Can you imagine the most important person in history addressing you personally? Would you listen to them or ignore them? Would you pay close attention and give heed to what they were saying?

The Bible is God speaking. It is given for specific reasons, but most of all, it gives us the opportunity to sit in His presence and hear from Him. Everything we need to know about everything we need to know about is found there. He has things He wants to talk to us about every single day.

---

[1] Colossians 3:16

[2] 2 Timothy 3:16–17

[3] https://pastorrick.com/god-wants-you-to-do-not-just-to-hear Feb. 24, 2022.

A Living Book

The Scripture is not merely a collection of static words on some pages. God reminds us it is dynamic because of its origin and nature.

> For the word of God is living and active and sharper than any two-edged sword, and piercing as far as the division of soul and spirit, of both joints and marrow, and able to judge the thoughts and intentions of the heart. And there is no creature hidden from His sight, but all things are open and laid bare to the eyes of Him with whom we have to do. [4]

When you sit with the Bible in your lap and have a heart ready to hear, the Spirit will bring it to life. Only God could do this, and He does.

Millions of believers have given testimony of this experience. Humble farmers, brilliant theologians, young students, and uneducated men and women have all experienced God's voice communing with them as they prayerfully read the Bible. This has happened across the world for generations. The Father loves to talk to all of His children.

Since the Word is one of His primary means of speaking to us, we must *cooperate*. We must draw near every day to read and study, memorize and meditate on His Word to know Him more and more. As we approach the Scripture, it is not just to gain knowledge but to encounter Him.

I've had this poem on the wall of my study for over thirty years as a reminder. It directs the way I approach the Scripture, for experience has proven it true. The belief that I can find Him on every page of His Word makes my heart soar.

I read Thy word, O Lord, each passing day,
And in thy sacred page find glad employ.
But this I pray: save from the killing letter.
Teach my heart, set free from human forms
The holy art of reading Thee in every line;
In precept, prophecy, and sign.
Till all my vision filled with Thee,
Thy likeness shall reflect in me.
Not knowledge, but Thyself my joy,
For this I pray.[5]

A Presence Centered Missionary

---

4 Hebrews 4:12–13

5 J.C. Macaulay, "Thyself"

As I was writing this book, a wonderful missionary in our church spoke to me.

"I think I'm supposed to tell you something, but I've hesitated."

"Why?" I asked.

"Well, I didn't want to seem proud or that I have everything all together, because I certainly don't. But the more you speak of abiding in God's presence, the more I feel compelled to tell you this story.

"When my husband and I first went to our missionary assignment, I was homeschooling my three children, trying to learn a difficult language, and acclimating to a new culture. I wanted to be there, but it was hard.

"One day a veteran missionary came up and asked me a probing question.

"How are you learning to practice the presence of God every day?"

"That's all he said, but it went like a knife through my heart. So, I began to ask the Lord to help me practice His presence. I had no idea how to begin.

"We were helping our children memorize Scripture every day and I was learning the verses with them. The next morning as I looked at the verses, the Lord spoke to my heart. I realized He just wanted me to concentrate on the first line of the verses we were learning.

"'Lord, I can memorize the whole passage,' I said to Him.

"'No,' I felt Him saying. 'You don't understand. I want you to slow down and listen to what I want to say to you through the first line.'

"The Lord kept me on that first line for two months! Like a prism turning in the light, I began to see more and more in that one verse. I couldn't think about anything else. Whenever my mind was in neutral, it would run to that line as I meditated on its truth and the Father and I discussed it together.

"And then one day," she said with tears in her eyes, "The Lord brought a dear native woman to me. She needed every single thing the Father had shown me in those two months as He and I had discussed that one line! And I shared it all with her, and it helped her greatly.

"And then I heard the Lord say, 'Now, let's go to the second line!'"

Then this precious missionary who had been so powerfully used by God in so many lives said to me. "I've been doing this now for 25 years. It's how I stay in His presence all day long."

Communing. This was how she was abiding in Christ, sitting at His feet, listening to Him continually, remaining in His presence. She was letting the Word of Christ richly dwell within her and aggressively looking for her next assignment to share it with others.

DAILY STUDY

PLANT A SEED

Read and begin to memorize ...

Colossians 3:16 | Let the word of Christ richly ____________ within you.

DIG DEEPER

According to the following verse, what will regular intake of the Word of God do for us? (Underline each result found in this verse)

> All Scripture is inspired [God-exhaled] by God and profitable for teaching, for reproof, for correction, for training in righteousness; so that the man of God may be adequate, equipped for every good work.

Which of these things have you experienced?

When you read and study God's Word, does it seem like just a book to you, or do you feel you are communing with God? Why does it feel that way to you?

How could you approach the Bible in a way that would lead to greater, more intimate communion with the Father?

What did you learn from the story of the missionary?

WRAP IT UP

Summarize what God seems to be saying to you today. What is your one-sentence takeaway?

TALK TO HIM

Spend time in prayer. Pray specifically about what you learned today.

DAY 3:
COMMUNING THROUGH UNCEASING PRAYER

I attended college during the Jesus Movement in the early 1970s. It was an unusual season of God's presence. It touched our campus, and it touched me. I was aggressively pursuing God and enjoying His presence, but there was one verse that really bothered me because it was not my experience. In fact, I questioned whether it was possible, but I knew it must be because it was from the inerrant word of God. So, I began to ask the Lord to help me experience this verse. And I have prayed about it continually ever since. The verse is simple:

> Pray without ceasing.[1]

Without ceasing? All the time? I knew God could not ask me to do something that I couldn't do by His grace. I knew there was no demand made upon my life that was not made upon the Christ who lived within me, but as I tried to pray continually throughout the day, I found it very difficult because of the distractions. Like a kid in a candy shop, I found that I was often lured away and would forget to pray.

It has taken years, but more and more (and certainly not perfectly) I have learned that unceasing prayer is not only possible, it is one of the primary keys to a Presence-centered life. God has given us several types of prayer to help us enjoy unbroken communion with Him.

DAILY STUDY

Read and begin to memorize …

1 Thessalonians 5:17 | Pray without ceasing.

---

[1] 1 Thessalonians 5:17

DIG DEEPER

What is the closest you have ever come to a day of unceasing prayer? What prompted it? What kept you in prayer throughout that day?

Why do you think continual prayer is so hard to maintain?

What would be different about your life if you were in continual communion with God throughout the day? What would you have that you are not experiencing now?

Do you think God is interested in continual communion with you in prayer? Why or why not?

WRAP IT UP

Summarize what God seems to be saying to you today. What is your one-sentence takeaway?

TALK TO HIM

Spend time in prayer. Pray specifically about what you learned today.

DAY 4:
MORNING AND EVENING

God told the children of Israel to build a portable Tabernacle as they traveled to the Promised Land. This was to be in the center of their camp as a continual place of His presence. Every component of that Tabernacle showed them how to receive the cleansing necessary to enter God's presence by faith.

Outside the Holy of Holies was a small altar where incense—a symbol for prayer—was burned. Listen to its purpose.

> "You shall put this altar in front of the veil that is near the ark of the testimony, in front of the mercy seat that is over the ark of the testimony, where I will meet with you. Aaron shall burn fragrant incense on it; he shall burn it every morning when he trims the lamps. When Aaron trims the lamps at twilight, he shall burn incense. There shall be perpetual incense before the LORD throughout your generations." [1]

Morning and evening incense ... morning and evening prayer.

There is something about beginning and ending your day in prayer that frames the day. If you read the biographies of well-known Christian men and women, you will discover that almost all of them began their day with a deliberate, disciplined time with God in His Word and prayer and ended the day in thanksgiving.

The apostle John reminded us of the value of those times of communion, not just to us, but to heaven.

> When He had taken the book, the four living creatures and the twenty-four elders fell down before the Lamb, each one holding a harp and golden bowls full of incense, which are the prayers of the saints. [2]

Morning, Word-driven prayers set the day with God and equip you for what you will face. It will provide you with what someone you will encounter later in the day desperately needs. George Mueller would read His Bible and pray until he got his soul "happy in the Lord," reasoning that he was not ready to meet others until he had met with God.

I once asked Henry Blackaby, a mentor to me as to thousands of others, about his morning devotions. He told me that he would get up an hour early.

---

[1] Exodus 30:6–8

[2] Revelation 5:8

But soon, realizing that was not enough, he got up an hour earlier ... and then another.

Finally, he simply resolved to rise whenever God awakened him. I was with him on many occasions when I noticed his notes as he headed to the pulpit to preach. It might be a few lines written on a scratch pad from the hotel, the summary of what God had shown him that very morning. God was giving His servant daily bread to deliver to thousands of hungry people.

Any man or woman who pays the price to commune with God will be used by God. God will see to that. Here is a simple pattern for morning prayer.

1. **Draw near to God.** Spend time entering into His presence as Jesus instructs in Matthew 6:6. Walk into the throne room and shut the door on every distraction. Then turn and face the throne and "pray to your Father." Stay in these moments of worship until you know you have become consciously aware of His presence. Reading the psalms, singing, or listening to worship music is often helpful. Most importantly, turn your attention to Him. Remove other distractions till He fills your vision.

   Spend time in humble consecration, admitting your sins and acknowledging your need, just as the priests did as they approached the presence of God in the "ark of the LORD God of Israel ."[3]

2. **Read the Word *experientially*.** Go to the Scripture readings for the day with a prayer that God will open your eyes and help you see wonderful things from His Word.[4] Read the Bible with a notebook in hand to record all that God says to you. Meditate on what God is communicating. Make application to your own life and commit to respond in whatever ways God directs. Make your goal to hear from God, not just get through a passage.

3. **Pray the Scripture *in*.** Remember, you are there to have a conversation with the Father, to enjoy His presence, and learn from Him. He *will* speak, and as He does, you want to retain what He communicates. The best ways to retain are to write it down and pray it in! (The helpful book, *Praying the Bible,* by Donald Whitney can help with this.[5]) Spend extended time in prayer for whatever God prompts you. Using prayer lists or cards can be helpful to remember needs.

---

[3] 1 Chronicles 15:12-15

[4] Psalm 119:18

[5] Donald Whitney, *Praying the Bible*, Donald Whitney, Crossway, Wheaton, IL, 2015

4. **Memorize a scripture** that God has made precious to you. Meditate on it throughout the day. Write it on a card and place it where you can see it daily. Let it "richly dwell within you."

5. **Be ready to join God in sharing truth.** Ask the Lord to bring someone across your path who might need what He shows you, and ask Him to open your mouth boldly to share with them. Realize that it was for this purpose that He has given you this understanding—not only for your good but also for others.

   My missionary friend asks God every day who He has on the agenda to share His truth with. It is amazing, but not surprising, how many spiritual conversations she has almost every week. Her life is a constant adventure. She often says to us, "God just must love me best to give me such an exciting life!" But her Presence-centered life is available to anyone.

Evening prayer brings your heart back to the Father, giving thanks for all He has done. Rehearse the blessings of the day and pray for His protection through the night hours. Often, these evening prayers are a wonderful way to join as a family in prayer.

DAILY STUDY

PLANT A SEED

Read and begin to memorize …

1 Thessalonians 5:17 | Pray without ___________.

DIG DEEPER

Do you have a habit, a rhythm for how you spend time in God's Word and prayer? Describe it.

Which of these things hinder you from establishing set time for you with God in the Word and prayer?

- ☐ I don't see the value.
- ☐ I don't prioritize this time.

- ☐ I don't prepare for it.
- ☐ When the time comes, I value sleep or other things more than meeting with God.
- ☐ When I try to meet with God, my mind begins to wander and I get distracted.
- ☐ I'll be honest, I'm not sure I know how to spend concentrated time with God.
- ☐ I don't think God really wants to meet with me?

Meeting with God in the mornings begins the night before. Sometimes there are unavoidable hindrances to this (a sick child, a work schedule, etc.). How can we compensate for such times so we don't lose this precious essential "morning or evening" routine?

What adjustments do you need to make this week to begin to make this stronger in your life?

Over the next three days, seek to set this fresh routine in your life. Ask God for His help in this. Remember, His presence is your greatest need and your presence is His great desire.

WRAP IT UP

Summarize what God seems to be saying to you today. What is your one-sentence takeaway?

TALK TO HIM

Spend time in prayer. Pray specifically about what you learned today.

DAY 5:
EVERYTHING PRAYER

Another way to pray without ceasing and to abide in His presence is to do what a favorite scripture in Philippians commands.

> Be anxious for nothing, but in *everything* by prayer and supplication with thanksgiving let your requests be made known to God. And the peace of God, which surpasses all comprehension, will guard your hearts and your minds in Christ Jesus. [1]

Did you worry about anything last week? Yesterday? Were you worried, bothered, anxious, upset? These are all signs that you were not practicing "everything prayer." There is only one possible way to be "anxious for nothing," and that is to "pray about everything!" You may think the word "everything" is an exaggeration, but it is not. It is the Word of God to us that comes straight from the One who knows us best and loves us most.

It can be done and must be done if we're going to live a Presence-centered life. In fact, it may be the single most important secret to such unceasing intimacy. What if every conversation you had today, every meeting, every decision, every relaxed moment, or season of hard work was laced with prayer? What if you were thanking God for *everything*, as Paul directs?

The secret to David's intimacy with Christ was this continual prayer, as he mentioned in Psalm 16, writing about the value of God's presence: "I have set the LORD *continually* before me."[2]

His fellow psalmist, Asaph, reminds us of this practice when he tells of bringing the ark of God back into Jerusalem: "Seek the Lord and His strength. Seek His face *continually*."[3]

Children understand this. When they are afraid, hungry, hurting, or simply need the warmth of intimacy, what do they do? They seek the face of their mom or dad. Nothing else will substitute for the joy and comfort that comes from a parent's face.

If you want to be continually aware of God's intimate presence, carry on a continuous conversation with Him. Enter His presence, draw near, and

---

[1] Philippians 4:6–7 *(emphasis mine)*

[2] Psalm 16:8 *(emphasis mine)*

[3] 1 Chronicles 16:11 *(emphasis mine)*

seek His face continually. You will discover that the smallest details of your life are important to Him, for it is the details and your willingness to bring them to Him that usher you into His presence. And, His presence is our greatest need and our presence is His great desire.

Intensive Prayer

There are also moments that call for a dramatic increase in prayer. Jesus said that there are some things that don't happen but by prayer and fasting.[4] Jesus would often pull away and spend an entire night in prayer. Greater demands call for greater prayer. You will find that intensive times of prayer (which may be hard but are essential) actually make your schedule easier because more is accomplished in such times than through any other means.

If you serve with a team, gather weekly for unhindered prayer and schedule a day of prayer each month. You will be astounded at what will happen and how much is accomplished in the presence of God. God is waiting for you there and such days of prayer will build the unity of your team in ways that nothing else can do.

DAILY STUDY

PLANT A SEED

Read and begin to memorize …

1 Thessalonians 5:17 | _______ without ceasing.

DIG DEEPER

How often do you worry?

- o Every day
- o Almost constantly
- o Occasionally, when there is an overwhelming issue
- o Almost never

---

4 Matthew 17:21

Read Philippians 4:4-6. What is the connection between worry and prayer?

Look at these verses. What do they teach us about the Lord's concern for everything in our lives?

> For though the Lord is exalted,
> Yet He regards the lowly,
> But the haughty He knows from afar.
> Though I walk in the midst of trouble, You will revive me;
> You will stretch forth Your hand against the wrath of my enemies,
> And Your right hand will save me.
> The Lord will accomplish what concerns me;
> Your lovingkindness, O Lord, is everlasting;
> Do not forsake the works of Your hands.[5]

Why would you think God would be interested in talking with you about everything? What benefit would such constant communication be to you? To Him?

---

[5] Psalms 138:6–8

Ask the Lord today to help you experience "everything prayer." At the end of the day, record what this experience was like.

WRAP IT UP

Summarize what God seems to be saying to you today. What is your one-sentence takeaway?

TALK TO HIM

Spend time in prayer. Pray specifically about what you learned today.

GROUP DISCUSSION

GETTING STARTED

This week we are studying one of the most essential "ways" of a Presence centered life. Remember, this "Abiding Wheel" diagram that we're learning is a tool we can use to help us enter and maintain a continual, daily awareness of God's presence. Also, it can be a great tool for discipling and mentoring others.

What touched you in your reading and study this week?

WATCH

As you're watching the video, write any thoughts that strike you for discussion with the group afterward.

DISCUSS

Don't feel like you have to get to every question. Let the Lord guide your conversation.

If you could have what you desire, what do you wish your communing with God would look like in a normal day? (Be specific) What steps could be taken to establish this rhythm?

What did you learn from the story of the missionary? What is your takeaway? (Re-read the story to the group if some have not heard it yet.)

Why do you think continual prayer is so hard to maintain?

Do you think unceasing prayer is possible? Why or why not?

What would be different about your life if you were in continual communion with God throughout the day? What would you have that you are not experiencing now?

Share with your group any of the things that have helped you become more consistent and fruitful in continual communication with God through the Word and prayer.

PRAY

Spend some time praying these truths in as a group. (Remind the group to do their daily study for next week.)

WEEK 7

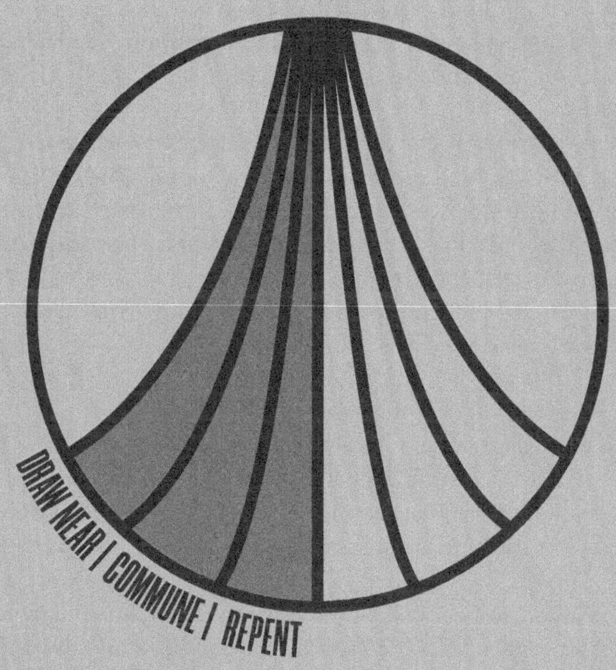

REPENT

DAY 1:

EVERYONE NEEDS IT

OF ALL THE GODLY MEN and women in history, the shepherd-king of Israel, David, may have lived the most Presence-centered life. He had learned God's ways as he tended sheep on the hillsides near Bethlehem where he came to know the Good Shepherd deeply. He knew how to draw near and commune. He had a matured faith early in life, and enough confidence in God to take on a giant that intimidated the entire Hebrew army.

God Himself said that David was a "man after My own heart." David did not turn from God even when betrayed by his familiar friend, Saul, or facing his darkest days. He understood God's purposes and embraced His sovereignty. He knew God would exalt him at the right time, and he humbly waited. Only a man who is intimate with God would make such choices.

David expressed his Presence-centered life through the many psalms that he wrote, which is why they are a treasure to every man and woman who hungers after God.

> How lovely are Your dwelling places, O Lord of hosts!
> ... How blessed are those who dwell in Your house!
> ... For a day in Your courts is better than a thousand outside.
> ... I would rather stand at the threshold of the house of my God
> Than dwell in the tents of wickedness. [1]

But David was not perfect. Satan was waiting with just the right distraction at the right time. At a moment when David should have been busy with the work of the King, he took a break. David and those around him probably thought this inactivity was harmless.

In this vulnerable position one night, he looked over from the high vantage point of his rooftop and saw a woman bathing. He had left the presence of God, and so he had no spiritual protection. If he heard it at all, he ignored God's voice. This careless moment of distraction led to adultery and murder. A whole string of sins occurred when David moved away from intimacy with God. He describes the next season of his life—away from God's presence—in Psalm 32.

> When I kept silent about my sin, my body wasted away
> Through my groaning all day long.
> For day and night, Your hand was heavy upon me;

[1] Psalm 84:1, 4, 10

My vitality was drained away as with the fever heat of summer. [2]

When he walked away from God, David was a mess. He experienced physical, emotional, and spiritual deterioration. To have known deep intimacy with the Father and then become distant through foolish choices is always tragic. It is miserable to lose the most valuable part of life—everything that matters and lasts. Spurgeon said it best:

> God's hand is very helpful when it uplifts, but it is awful when it presses down. Better a world on your shoulders like Atlas than God's hand on your heart like David's.[3]

After days of sin and guilt (we don't know how long), David came to his senses and realized what he had done. He then exhibited another essential "way" of a Presence-centered life.

David repented.

DAILY STUDY

PLANT A SEED

Read and begin to memorize …

Acts 24:16 | In view of this, I also do my best to maintain always a blameless conscience both before God and before men.

DIG DEEPER

Describe a time when you were wandering from God and He placed His strong hand of conviction on you. What did it feel like? What were the results?

[2] Psalm 32:3–4

[3] Charles Spurgeon, *Treasury of David*, Charles Spurgeon, Psalm 51.

When you have remained in an unrepentant state, did you notice any of these effects? (Describe all that apply).

- ☐ *Physical* effects
  What were they like?

- ☐ *Emotional* effects
  What were they like?

- ☐ *Spiritual* effects
  What were they like?

In your understanding, what is repentance? Write your definition.

Why do you think repentance is essential to abiding daily in the presence of God?

WRAP IT UP

Summarize what God seems to be saying to you today. What is your one-sentence takeaway?

TALK TO HIM

Spend time in prayer. Pray specifically about what you learned today.

DAY 2:
REPENTANCE TOWARD GOD

When I was a boy, there was a man who walked the downtown streets of our city with a double-sided signboard draped over his body. On one side, it said, "REPENT!" and on the other, "TURN OR BURN!" I always appreciated his boldness, but it left me with only one thought about the beautiful gift of repentance.

Repentance FROM

Repentance literally means a "change of mind." We were thinking one way, but something has happened to show us the error of that thought.

Most people, even unbelievers, can recognize that something is wrong, but not have biblical, godly repentance. A humanistic response to our sin merely comes from humanistic ideas and will always produce a shallow, temporary repentance, but with little turning. Spurgeon said the following:

> There is a repentance that is fatally flawed because it is not toward God. In some, there is a repentance of sin that is produced by a sense of *shame* … Others exhibit a repentance that consists entirely of *horror* at the future punishment of sin. But if such persons could be assured that no punishment would follow, they would continue in sin and not only be content to live in it but be delighted to have it so.[4]

Repentance TOWARD

Lasting repentance always has a different destination. It is not just repenting "from" sin, but "toward" God, as Paul preached.

> I testified to both Jesus and Greeks of repentance *toward* God and faith in our Lord Jesus.[5]

Genuine repentance is a Spirit-wrought conviction that we are missing the greatest thing … that we have lost the sense of His presence as we have turned to other gods. We vainly think those gods will satisfy, which is always a lie. Recognizing the loss and all it means, we turn back to Him and naturally, gladly re-enter His presence. We see our sin as God sees it, say about it what He says, and respond to it like God responds.

Remember: these distractions we have followed may not look too bad (like

---

[4] Spurgeon Study Bible, CSB, Holman, Nashville, TN., 2017

[5] Acts 20.21 *(emphasis mine)*

Martha's sins), but they are deadly in that they have pulled us away from God's presence.

We must turn and look to Him and Him alone as our sole source. We realize He is the Vine, we are the branches, and we can do nothing apart from Him. "I have no good besides You," David said, and so here was his repentance, "I will set the Lord continually before me" (Psalm 16:2, 8). The wise King saw something of extraordinary value—the pearl of great price—and so he turned deliberately, humbly, and fully.

The repentant who enjoy God gain everything for everything flows from His presence. Repentance is not a terrible, hard step when viewed this way, but the beautiful entrance to all that matters and lasts.

DAILY STUDY

PLANT A SEED

Read, fill in the blanks and try to memorize, reciting it multiple times ...

Acts 24:16 | In view of this, I also do my best to maintain always a blameless ______________ both before God and before men.

DIG DEEPER

Do you have some sins that you know are wrong but have a hard time getting rid of in your life? What do you think makes these so hard to overcome?

Do you feel you have been turning "toward" God or merely "from" sin? How effective has that been?

Think of 2-3 of your toughest areas of sin. Make a list of all the things that you are missing when you hold onto these sins.

What step(s) could you begin to take in cooperation with God to be free from these sins and recognize the value of returning to God's presence?

WRAP IT UP

Summarize what God seems to be saying to you today. What is your one-sentence takeaway?

TALK TO HIM

Spend time in prayer. Pray specifically about what you learned today.

DAY 3:
THE BEAUTY OF GENUINE REPENTANCE

My brother-in-law, Bailey Smith, was a pastor. He once bought a broken-down 1931 Chevrolet. His dream was to restore it one day, but it was a constant source of irritation to my sister, Sandy, as it sat in their yard for over a decade. Finally, Bailey had the resources to begin the restoration process.

He called me one day and invited me to his garage. Positioning me outside the garage door, he opened it with a flourish. The door flew up and revealed the most beautiful car you could imagine—original paint colors and trim, original interior, new engine. Everything was restored to the manufacturer's original specifications.

Bailey's son, Scott, said:

> It took him eleven years total. He could have had it done much sooner but he wanted it all original. Every bolt and every screw was correct. The guy who helped with the restoration took most of the parts, cleaned the rust off, and rethreaded the bolts as he could. Re-chromed all the chrome pieces. Every piece was stripped to bare metal and painted. Period-correct mohair interior. It was way more exact and correct than it was probably worth. No key. No radio. Starter on the floor. Everything looked brand new and worked as new. It probably was not an exceptionally rare car, but it was exactly like it was when new.

God has a similar idea. We have been devastated by the fall. Sin has taken its toll on our lives. We have unsightly habits, humanistic ideas, we're horribly out of alignment with God's will, and we don't run right!

This doesn't deter the Father, for He has a plan and the means to accomplish it. He is intent on restoring us to the Manufacturer's original specifications, but we must cooperate. And He is deliberate down to the last detail in our lives.

> And we know that God causes all things to work together for good to those who love God, to those who are called according to His purpose. For those whom He foreknew, He also predestined to *become conformed to the image of His Son.*[6]

---

6 Romans 8:28–29, *(emphasis mine)*

As we walk in His presence, God begins to graciously show us everything in our lives that is not as it should be. The Holy Spirit in us continually convicts us of our sins and then provides the means for change as we rely upon Him.

The days of God's convicting work are good days. Hard days, but good. As He works in us, we realize that:

1. His convictions are an indication of His continued love for us.
2. We are about to experience a deeper deliverance.
3. Our release will equip us to help others who need the same rescue, opening up areas where we can join God in His work.
4. Repenting helps us experience less of ourselves so we can experience more of Christ.

As the Spirit opens our eyes to areas in need of change, we have several options. We can ignore his promptings. We can blame others or make excuses for our sins. We can rationalize or justify our weaknesses and failures or dig in our heels in rebellion. Continued days, weeks, and even years of resisting God's convictions can result in a calloused conscience. The Bible speaks of some men who are "seared in their own conscience as with a branding iron."[7] This is a dangerous practice, particularly if repeated continually. Right can become wrong to us, and we lose the ability to hear God's promptings. All that is best and essential for our lives will be lost, for everything flows from His presence.

Or we can agree with God and repent. Repentance is a change of mind. It is thinking differently … *I thought the way I was responding was good or beneficial. Now I see it is not. I agree with God's evaluation, and I gladly turn to Him in honest confession and rely on Him for cleansing and the grace to choose another path.*

Genuine repentance brings us to a godly sorrow that Paul speaks about to the Corinthians—

> I now rejoice, not that you were made sorrowful, but that you were made sorrowful to the point of repentance; for you were made sorrowful according to the will of God, so that you might not suffer loss in anything through us. For the sorrow that is according to the will of God produces a repentance without regret, leading to salvation, but the sorrow of the world produces death. For behold what earnestness this very thing, this godly sorrow, has produced in you: what vindication of yourselves, what indignation, what fear, what longing, what zeal, what avenging of wrong! In everything you demonstrated yourselves to be innocent in the matter. [8]

We must see repentance as a normal, essential, and constant process in a Presence-centered life. It should happen regularly and effortlessly and spring from

---

[7] 1 Timothy 4:2

[8] 2 Corinthians 7:9–11

a continual desire to walk closer and closer with the One who loves us perfectly and knows exactly what we need. If we want to abide in His presence, we must be lifelong repenters.

DAILY STUDY

PLANT A SEED

Read, fill in the blanks, and try to memorize, reciting it multiple times …

Acts 24:16 | In view of this, I also do my best to maintain always a blameless conscience both before ______ and before ______.

DIG DEEPER

Where are the areas of your life that need the most work to "restore you to the Manufacturer's original specifications"?

Please read the following list again, deliberately considering how God wants you to turn from your toughest sins and toward His presence.

1. His convictions are an indication of His continued love for me.
2. I am about to experience a deeper deliverance.
3. My release will equip me to help others who need the same rescue, opening up areas where I can join God in His work.
4. Repenting helps me experience less of myself so I can experience more of Christ.

Do you believe what you just read? If not, ask God to convince you of those truths. Ask Him to help you begin to see the beauty and joy of genuine repentance.

How could repentance in these areas equip you to help others? What do you think God wants to do in these areas of your life? How could God use you if these areas became sins of your past, not present?

What would you love to see Him do? Write your response as a prayer …

WRAP IT UP

Summarize what God seems to be saying to you today. What is your one-sentence takeaway?

TALK TO HIM

Spend time in prayer. Pray specifically about what you learned today.

DAY 4:
MAJOR REPENTANCE

Sometimes we need a season of significant and deep repentance. A prolonged absence from God's presence can leave a tangled web of sins that must be addressed and resolved.

This was critical for my life at age seventeen when I returned to the Lord after a time of rebellion. My father encouraged me to do a simple, practical exercise that he had learned from the missionary, Bertha Smith, who was in the Shantung Revival. This would become a practical means of repentance that I would continue for the rest of my life.

At his prompting, I took some paper and wrote the words "Sin List" at the top. I prayed the prayer of David: "Search me, O God, and know my heart. Try me and know my anxious thoughts and see if there be any hurtful way in me, and lead me in the everlasting way."[9]

I then asked the Lord to show me anything in my life that was not right with Him or others. I circled the issues where I knew I would need to go to someone and clear my conscience. I didn't argue with God, blame Him or others, or make excuses. I just wrote down everything He brought to mind. When I finished, I had seven pages filled, front and back!

At my father's counsel, I then began going to people I'd wronged, asking their forgiveness. My words were not elaborate: *I'm trying to get right with God and others, and I've realized that what I did or said was wrong. Would you forgive me?* No one refused. In fact, many sought my forgiveness also. But when I finished that exercise, I was overwhelmed with joy! It was not that I had not sinned, but I knew that I had sought, as far as it lay within me, to make all things right.

Paul always sought to maintain a clear conscience in two directions, and it is the way of a Presence-centered man or woman. "In view of this, I also do my best to maintain always a blameless conscience both before God and before men."[10]

Norman Grubb was a missionary involved in a nationwide revival in Rwanda that lasted twenty years. He wrote about his experiences in the little booklet *Continuous Revival.*[11] When he was asked how this unusual season of God's presence was maintained, he said they "kept the roof off and the walls down"—nothing between themselves and God and nothing between themselves and others.

---

[9] Psalm 139:23–24

[10] Acts 24:16

[11] Norman Grubb, *Continuous Revival*, Norman Grubb, CLC Publications, Fort Washington, PA.

DAILY STUDY

PLANT A SEED

Read, fill in the blanks and try to memorize, reciting it multiple times …

Acts 24:16 | In view of this, I also do my best to ____________ always a blameless conscience both before God and before men.

DIG DEEPER

Today is an important day of application. Spend sufficient time on this exercise. It will help you learn the process of repentance.

1. Spend deliberate time working through the "Repentance Worksheet below."
2. Begin the process of clearing your conscience with anyone you've wronged. If you need help with this, get some godly counsel. You can also read my small booklet, *Lifting Life's Greatest Load: How to Gain and Maintain a Clear Conscience* at https://billelliff.org/products/lifting-lifes-greatest-load.

REPENTANCE WORKSHEET

"If we say that we have no sin, we are deceiving ourselves and the truth is not in us. If we confess our sins, He is faithful and righteous to forgive us our sins and to cleanse us from all unrighteousness" (1 John 1:8-9; NASB*).*

Begin with a prayer like this:
Father, search my heart and show me my sin and need. I will agree with You and ask You to cleanse from me the sin of . . . *(underline all that apply)*:

- Pride, bragging, making sure I'm "known;" taking credit for my success; love of human praise; a secret fondness to be noticed; love of supremacy; love of reputation; a desire to achieve regardless of the methods; drawing attention to myself in conversations
- Anger, impatience; a touchy, sensitive spirit; resentment and retaliation when I am disapproved of or contradicted; sharp, harsh words; rudeness; sarcasm; a stubborn, unteachable spirit; an arguing, talkative spirit; contention; an unyielding, headstrong disposition; a driving, commanding spirit; a desire to control most circumstances and people; a drive to win every argument; a desire to always be seen as "right" or come out on top; inflexibility (things have to go my way); unapproachableness; resenting or resisting the authorities God has placed

over me; resisting or rebelling against God's providence or ways as He seeks to develop my life

- A desire to criticize and point out flaws when I'm set aside or unnoticed; gossip, criticism; focusing on the failures of others; unkind responses; spreading strife; being envious or jealous of others; withdrawing or ignoring others out of a secret desire to retaliate; lack of real love; treating people as objects
- Dishonesty, lying; exaggeration; evading and covering the truth; leaving a better impression of myself than is strictly true; covering up my real faults; defensiveness; an unwillingness to accept responsibility for my sin; pitching blame on others
- Fear; a man-fearing, man-pleasing spirit; shrinking from duty; passivity; worry about whether every-thing will come out all right; lack of quiet confidence in God; lack of gratitude; unbelief; doubting God's goodness; worry and complaining in the midst of difficulty
- Laziness; wasting time (often with the Internet, television, games, etc.); gluttony; overindulgence; drunkenness; being a stumbling block to others because of my habits; abuse of drugs (including prescription drugs); a tendency to trust medication more than God; lust, pornography, adultery, fornication, incest, abortion, sodomy
- Materialism; loving things more than loving God or others; always wanting more; buying things I don't need; not giving; robbing God of His tithes and offerings; stinginess; worry over my finances; living beyond what God has provided; excessive debt; an unwillingness to admit and correct my misuse of God's money
- Unforgiveness; bitterness and hatred toward those who have hurt me; an unwillingness to clear my conscience with others; intolerance of others; bigotry, prejudice; harbored hurt
- Deadness and formality; lack of concern for lost people; not sharing my faith with others; dryness and indifference; lukewarmness and apathy; insensitivity toward others; unwillingness to serve (a consumer mentality); a desire to be served; self-centeredness; hypocrisy; disobedience to God's promptings; lack of time with God in His Word; little interest in intimacy with God; prayerlessness; unwillingness to let God have control
- Also *(list anything else God brings to mind)*:

After you have agreed with God and confessed these sins:

- **Claim** God's promise at the top and thank Him for His forgiveness, made possible by the cross!
- **Turn** in full repentance and a desire for Christ's complete lordship in your life.
- **Clear your conscience** by seeking forgiveness from any people you've wronged … and do it now!

WRAP IT UP

Summarize what God seems to be saying to you today. What is your one-sentence takeaway?

TALK TO HIM

Spend time in prayer. Pray specifically about what you learned today.

DAY 5:
IMMEDIATE REPENTANCE

More often, what is needed (and essential for maintaining a Presence-centered life) is to practice daily, immediate confession. Every time the Holy Spirit convicts us of something that is wrong, we should instantly agree and repent. The Christian life is not a matter of sinless perfection, but immediate confession. When this becomes one of our common practices, we will have found a key to abiding in God's presence.

A glorious side benefit of immediate confession is the humility that it brings. Letting God have a conversation with us about our sins and not ignoring but agreeing with Him is a glorious and constant reminder of our need for Him. The cover-all prayer of "Lord, forgive me of all of my sins" is often not effective and can be a sidestep to keep us from facing the realities that need to be adjusted in our lives. We must let the Father be specific with us. We must embrace the process if we are to remain in His presence and grow into His likeness.

This is why it is so important for us as parents to teach our children to deal with their sins properly and to seek to clear their conscience with others, particularly their siblings. Our daily work with them is teaching them a spiritual "way" they will use with God and others for the rest of their lives.

We should see God's continual reproof and conviction as one of the most beautiful evidences of His care for us. He is lovingly training us, and to do so, He must help us overcome our faults.

> "For whom the Lord loves He disciplines…" All discipline for the moment seems not to be joyful but sorrowful, yet to those who have been trained by it, afterward, it yields the peaceful fruit of righteousness.[12]

Repentance is a godly man's humble, knowing response to God's training. It yields a growth that nothing else can accomplish. This is one of the essential ways of a Presence-centered life.

PLANT A SEED

Read and ask God to help you share this verse with someone today.

[12] Hebrews 12:6,11

DAILY STUDY

Acts 24:16 | In view of this, I also do my best to maintain always a blameless conscience both before God and before men.

DIG DEEPER

Today's exercise is simple. Throughout the day, seek to remain in God's presence through these two steps:

- Each time you sin, turn to God as quickly as you notice it and immediately repent. Ask Him to show you—right at that moment—what you were missing as you turned away from His presence. Ask for His cleansing.
- If someone else is involved, courageously and humbly go to them immediately and ask for their forgiveness. This may happen multiple times during the day (even with the same person), but your quick response will help teach a lesson and begin to build a lifestyle of repentance before God and man.

WRAP IT UP

Summarize what God seems to be saying to you today. What is your one-sentence takeaway?

TALK TO HIM

Spend time in prayer. Pray specifically about what you learned today.

GROUP DISCUSSION

GETTING STARTED

This week's study of the way of repentance is where some can easily stop in their spiritual growth. They do not realize what God is doing and how important it is in their experience of God's presence. I hope you worked deeply and thoroughly through the "Repentance Worksheet." If you haven't yet, please don't neglect it. If you have questions about what to do, please seek the help of someone whose spiritual leadership you trust.

What was most helpful about your personal study this week?

What was your experience like as you worked through the "Repentance Worksheet?"

WATCH

As you're watching the video, write any thoughts that strike you for discussion with the group afterward.

DISCUSS

Don't feel like you have to get to every question. Let the Lord guide your conversation.

In your best understanding, what is repentance and why is it essential to abiding daily in the presence of God?

What do you think of Paul use of the phrase "repentance *toward* God?" Why did he say that instead of merely "repentance *away from* sin?"[13]

Why do you think repentance is so hard at times?

We turn away from God because we think something else is more valuable. What are some of the ways that God wants to use to bring us back to His presence?

Read through this list aloud in your group. Are these things true about repentance? Discuss why this is important to understand.

1. His convictions are an indication of His continued love for me.
2. I am about to experience a deeper deliverance.
3. My release will equip me to help others who need the same rescue, opening up areas where I can join God in His work.
4. Repenting helps me experience less of myself so I can experience more of Christ.

Talk about your experiences this week of learning to live a Presence-centered life and how central repentance is to this. If there is some area you really need to share with the group and get their help and prayers, now is the best time to take that step.

PRAY

Spend some time praying these truths in as a group. (Remind the group to do their daily study for next week.

[13] Acts 20:21

WEEK 8

BE FILLED

DAY 1:
GREATER WORKS

THINK OF WHAT THE FIRST DISCIPLES experienced when they were with Jesus. Imagine hearing the wisdom from His mouth, feeling overwhelmed by His perfect acceptance, and watching a flesh-and-blood man filled with the full power of God.

Imagine what it must have been like to be constantly challenged by His heavenly vision and humbled by the purity of His motivations. We've never been around anyone who was totally unselfish, completely humble, absolutely pure. But they were. This was why they followed Him.

And imagine how the vision of a new kingdom must have filled their souls. They became so enamored with His thoughts of the new order He was establishing that they left everything to follow Him.

This was why the cross was so devastating to them. They believed that He was the Son of God and assumed He was indestructible—until they saw Him mangled by a Roman whip and nailed to a bloody cross. The loss seemed devastating, for they had given their lives to building His new order. The personal loss was beyond description, for they had never been loved in such a way.

For three days, they mourned until one of the followers came running into the room, proclaiming that He had risen. Later, when the resurrected Christ appeared to them, they began to understand more and more of what would occur. They watched Him ascend to heaven in a cloud while charging them to remain in Jerusalem and wait for what the Father had promised. Jesus said,

> "John baptized with water, but you will be baptized with the Holy Spirit not many days from now … You will receive power when the Holy Spirit has come upon you; and you shall be My witnesses both in Jerusalem, and in all Judea and Samaria, and even to the remotest part of the earth."[1]

And so they waited and prayed until the day of Pentecost. They were all together in one place when that moment came.

> And suddenly, there came from heaven a noise like a violent rushing wind, and it filled the whole house where they were sitting. And there appeared to them tongues as of fire distributing themselves, and they rested on each one of them. *And they were all filled with the Holy Spirit.*[2]

---

[1] Acts 1:5–8

[2] Acts 2:2–4, *(emphasis mine)*

Signs and wonders appeared, just as at Jesus' birth, to authenticate the entry of a new age. They spoke the gospel with boldness, thousands were saved, and the church was born. But think of the foundation of this amazing experience—they were all *filled with God!* The Spirit of God had come to dwell in them. The same Christ. The same love. The same power was in them!

All that Christ was now resided in each of them. Everything they had experienced temporarily when they were around Christ, they now had permanently. As they yielded to Him, they experienced His life flowing through them like "rivers of living water," just as He had promised.

> "If anyone is thirsty, let him come to Me and drink. He who believes in Me, as the Scripture said, 'From his innermost being will flow rivers of living water.'" But this He spoke of the Spirit, whom those who believed in Him were to receive; for the Spirit was not yet given, because Jesus was not yet glorified. [3]

There would be no more temporary separation from His presence. He was not only near, but He was also living in them all day, every day. All they needed they had, for they had the indwelling Christ. They now had the means to experience His presence constantly, which is our greatest need.

DAILY STUDY

PLANT A SEED

Read and begin to memorize ...

Ephesians 5:18 | And do not get drunk with wine, for that is dissipation, but be filled with the Holy Spirit.

DIG DEEPER

The beautiful truth of the Holy Spirit's presence in every true believer (His *indwelling*) is the foundational key to godly living, yet we are often confused about this. Mark all the statements below that you think are true.

___The Holy Spirit is merely an influence
___The Holy Spirit is God Himself
___The Spirit comes to Christians occasionally
___The Spirit is always present in the believer

---

[3] John 7:37–39

___The filling of the Spirit happens only at special times
___The filling of the Spirit can be the constant experience of the believer
___We can be effective Christians without being filled by the Spirit
___The evidence of His filling are the fruits of the Spirit, listed in Galatians 5:22-23
___We are filled to feel good
___We are filled to be equipped for ministry

What do you think the disciples thought as they were filled with the Holy Spirit on the day of Pentecost? What was now different? (Read the account in Acts 2.)

What do you think Jesus meant when He said the following to His disciples right before His death?

> "Truly, truly, I say to you, he who believes in Me, the works that I do, he will do also; and greater works than these he will do; because I go to the Father." [4]

Why do you think it was necessary for God to indwell us by His Spirit?

[4] John 14:12

Why did Jesus describe the Holy Spirit as "rivers of living water" that would flow from the lives of believers?[5]

WRAP IT UP

Summarize what God seems to be saying to you today. What is your one-sentence takeaway?

TALK TO HIM

Spend time in prayer. Pray specifically about what you learned today.

---

5 John 7:37-39

DAY 2:

OVERWHELMING MISSION-ASTOUNDING POWER

The disciples knew they had a mission to be His witnesses, make disciples of all nations, and help bring in His new kingdom … all of that amid overwhelming persecution. But now, they had permanent help and power to accomplish the task. They possessed all the resources of heaven.

A recurring phrase indicates the Spirit's presence in them. This phrase is the explanation for the explosion of the early church.

> When they needed someone to preach, "then Peter, *filled with the Holy Spirit*, said to them "[6]
>
> When they needed someone to lead, "they chose Stephen, a man *full of faith and of the Holy Spirit*."[7]
>
> When they needed strength under persecution, "being *full of the Holy Spirit*, he gazed intently into heaven and saw the glory of God, and Jesus standing at the right hand of God."[8]
>
> When the persecuted Christians were afraid, … "and when they had prayed, the place where they had gathered together was shaken, and they were all *filled with the Holy Spirit* and began to speak the word of God with boldness."[9]
>
> And the continual testimony about the church was that "all the disciples were continually *filled with joy and with the Holy Spirit*."[10]

The Holy Spirit is mentioned fifty-nine times in the twenty-eight chapters of the Book of Acts. This glorious historical account of the early church could have been named "The Acts of the Holy Spirit," for that is what it records.

---

[6] Acts 4:8, *(emphasis mine)*

[7] Acts 6:5, *(emphasis mine)*

[8] Acts 7:55, *(emphasis mine)*

[9] Acts 4:31, *(emphasis mine)*

[10] Acts 13:52, *(emphasis mine)*

The rest of the New Testament both teaches and illustrates what the Holy Spirit does in and through His children who will cooperate with Him. It explains spiritual gifts that are given to us by God (the gifts of the Spirit), how we can walk by the Spirit, how we can also quench or grieve the Spirit, and how we can be filled continually by the Holy Spirit.

The Bible also shows us that the Body of Christ (the church) is only effective and powerful in its great mission when each member is filled with the Spirit. Remember, we were made like He is to join Him in His work.

The Spirit of God has come to indwell every believer, giving us access to the presence of God. His presence is our greatest need, and our presence is His great desire. As we are filled with Him, we become usable to Him for His glory and our good.

DAILY STUDY

PLANT A SEED

Read and memorize as you fill in the blanks …

Ephesians 5:18 | And do not get __________ with wine, for that is dissipation, but be __________ with the Holy Spirit.

DIG DEEPER

Right before He ascended to heaven, Jesus gave the small band of disciples an overwhelming mission to make disciples of all nations and to be His witnesses in Jerusalem, Judea, Samaria, and the remotest parts of the earth.[11]

- What might the disciples' reaction to this calling have been *before* the Holy Spirit came at Pentecost? What do you think they were saying to themselves and to one another?

- What do you think the disciples might have been saying to themselves and to one another *after* the Spirit descended at Pentecost?

[11] Matthew 28:18-20; Acts 1:8

Read Acts 2. What were some of the immediate results when all the disciples were filled with the Holy Spirit?

Read the following verse and explain what the filling of the Holy Spirit did for the believers in Acts.

> And when they had prayed, the place where they had gathered together was shaken, and they were all filled with the Holy Spirit and began to speak the word of God with boldness.[12]

Have you ever consciously thought about being filled with the Holy Spirit?

- ☐ Yes
- ☐ No
- ☐ I'm not sure

What do you think some of the obvious results would be if you were filled with the Spirit?

What do you think some of the obvious results would be if all of the believers in a church were filled with the Holy Spirit?

WRAP IT UP

Summarize what God seems to be saying to you today. What is your one-sentence takeaway?

TALK TO HIM

Spend time in prayer. Pray specifically about what you learned today.

---

[12] Acts 4:31

DAY 3:

AND NOW YOU!

Just as it was in the beginning of the church, the Spirit's presence and power is to be the continual experience for every believer and for the church. God gave a life-changing command to all of Christ's followers in every age:

"And do not get drunk with wine, for that is dissipation, but be filled with the Spirit."[13]

Obedience to this command will result in everything needed to fulfill our part of the mission, no matter our background, education, gifting, or personality..

The filling of the Holy Spirit is not to be an occasional experience for the follower of Christ. It is not unusual or ecstatic. It is to be our regular experience all day, every day, and is part of a presence-centered life.

What is the filling of the Spirit, and why is it so essential?

The filling of the Holy Spirit is the believer's conscious, continual choice to yield control to the Holy Spirit who lives within them.

Conscious

This filling does not happen without our agreement. It comes from the recognition that we need Someone else in control. The natural, unconscious position of every believer is for self to be in control. It's our standard operating procedure. It's the way all people normally live. Self-centered living leads to all that is wrong with this world. The word "flesh" in the Scripture refers to our normal humanity without God. We are to consciously turn from being filled with self—walking by the flesh—and be filled with the Spirit. The control of God's Spirit begins with the awareness of our desperate need.

DAILY STUDY

PLANT A SEED

Read and begin to memorize …

Ephesians 5:18 | And do not get drunk with __________, for that is dissipation, but be filled with the __________ Spirit.

[13] Ephesians 5.18

■ DIG DEEPER

What does this statement mean to you?

> "This filling does not happen without our agreement. It comes from the recognition that we need Someone else in control."

What helps us understand our need for the Spirit's filling? What leads us to desire His filling?

"Self-centered living leads to all that is wrong with this world." In what ways have you battled self-centeredness in your own life? (Examples could include stinginess with time or money, putting your own comfort ahead of others, entertaining thoughts of superiority, etc.)

What are some of the results when the Holy Spirit is *not* in control? (Be specific and give illustrations from your own experience).

What role do humility and brokenness (the surrender of our will to the will of God) play in the filling of the Holy Spirit?

WRAP IT UP

Summarize what God seems to be saying to you today. What is your one-sentence takeaway?

TALK TO HIM

Spend time in prayer. Pray specifically about what you learned today.

DAY 4:
A CONTINUAL CHOICE

Continual

God's command for us to follow His Spirit is continual: "be *being* filled." It indicates that something can stop or hinder this filling and that something is sin. Each time we are tempted or distracted and choose to ignore God, we take control again. We have chosen to walk after the flesh. The results are always disastrous, and so we must come again and yield to His control.

> Now the deeds of the flesh are evident, which are: immorality, impurity, sensuality, idolatry, sorcery, enmities, strife, jealousy, outbursts of anger, disputes, dissensions, factions, envying, drunkenness, carousing, and things like these.[14]

Throughout the day, we should repeatedly turn to the Spirit within us, ask Him to take control, and join Him in whatever He prompts us to do.

Choice

The filling of God's Spirit is a choice that is made possible by the grace of God. Paul would later say that we are to "walk by the Spirit," and if we do, we will "not carry out the desire of the flesh."[15]

All of us were dominated by the flesh before we came to Christ. The fruit of a fleshly life is described in Galatians 5:19-21 and none of it is good. But if we follow the Spirit, Paul says, we will see the fruit that the Spirit produces flowing through our lives.

> But the fruit of the Spirit is love, joy, peace, patience, kindness, goodness, faithfulness, gentleness, self-control.[16]

We must come to the end of ourselves and continually hunger for His presence and control, for His presence is our greatest need and our presence is God's great desire. When we find ourselves self-consumed, it is because we are not filled with Him and have lost the desire for His empowering. We think we can handle life on our own. We must return to the hunger that pursues His filling, and this is a choice. A Puritan prayer expresses this desire well:

---

[14] Galatians 5:19–21

[15] Galatians 5:16

[16] Galatians 5:22–23

O Lord God, I pray not so much for graces as for the Spirit Himself because I feel His absence and act by my own spirit in everything.

Give me not weak desires but the power of His presence, for this is the surest way to have all His graces.

Save me from great hindrances, from being content with a little measure of the Spirit, from thinking Thou wilt not give me more.

When I feel my lack of Him, light up life and faith, for when I lose Thee, I am either in the dark and cannot see Thee, or Satan and my natural abilities content me with a little light so that I seek no further for the Spirit of life.[17]

To Yield Control

Paul uses the illustration of drunkenness to make his point in Ephesians 5:18. He challenges us not to get drunk with wine because it leads to devastating excesses and foolishness. When a man is drunk, he is controlled by the drink. He does what the drink leads him to do. But we are to be controlled by the Spirit of God. As we consciously yield control to the Spirit and follow Him, we will do what the Spirit says, and it will yield what only God can give.

> But I say, walk by the Spirit, and you will not carry out the desire of the flesh. For the flesh sets its desire against the Spirit, and the Spirit against the flesh; for these are in opposition to one another.[18]

At any given moment, a believer is choosing to either follow the Spirit or himself. We cannot walk in two paths simultaneously. (Try it: Stand up and walk to your right. Then, reverse directions and walk to your left. Then, stand in the middle and try walking in both directions at the same time!) It's impossible to follow the Spirit and flesh at the same time. We're either on one path or the other. This is why every choice to be distracted and move from His presence demands us to return in repentance and choose again the filling of His Spirit.

As we repent of all known sins, we simply acknowledge God's presence in us and our glad willingness to let Him lead. We ask Him to take over, to fill us with Himself and then we walk in faith, trusting that He will do what He promised. We do not need to seek an emotional, supernatural feeling. In fact, this is not to be abnormal, but the normal state—the way—of the Presence-centered life. It is the daily pathway to enjoy His presence, and His presence is our greatest need.

---

[17] *The Valley of Vision: A Collection of Puritan Prayers and Devotions*, Banner of Truth Trust, Carlisle, PA, 2002, pg. 48-49.

[18] Galatians 5:16–17

DAILY STUDY

PLANT A SEED

Read this verse and continue to memorize it. And then take a moment to pray it in. Ask that God would do this in you right now.

Ephesians 5:18 | And do not get drunk with wine, for that is dissipation, but be filled with the Holy Spirit.

DIG DEEPER

What specific things in your life most often interrupt the filling of the Holy Spirit? (See Galatians 5:10-21)

What does it mean that we must consciously choose to be filled with the Holy Spirit? If we don't "consciously choose" what is the alternative?

Why is it so hard to "yield control" to the Holy Spirit?

We don't "run out" of the Spirit of God. He is the One who lives in us and He lives fully in us. But we can quench or grieve Him. We can choose to take control (almost unconsciously at times). At that point, what should we immediately do to continue to abide in His presence and be used by Him?

One man said, "It's not how much of the Spirit you have; it's how much of you does the Spirit have?" Pause and ask Him what areas need to come under His control. He is a perfect leader and will lead you in "all the right paths for His name's sake."[19] You can trust Him with all of your life—every area and every choice.

WRAP IT UP

Summarize what God seems to be saying to you today. What is your one-sentence takeaway?

TALK TO HIM

Spend time in prayer. Pray specifically about what you learned today.

[19] Psalm 23:3

DAY 5:
YOUR STORY

I came to know Christ early in life as a pastor's son, but I got distracted and wandered during my high school years. I strayed into much sin and rebellion, and I was miserable.

Finally, I began to try and live the Christian life. I tried and tried, but the harder I tried, the more I failed. God allowed me to continue in this "Bill Elliff-self-help plan" just long enough to bring me to desperation. One night, I finally came to the end of myself. I cried out, *Lord, if You want to do anything with my life, You're going to have to do it, because I can't!* It was almost as if I heard God rejoicing, for this surrender was what He was waiting for.

I went home to my parents and immediately and fully began to confess the sin in my life, as I shared in the previous chapter. My dad began to teach me that the Holy Spirit lived in me. That, if I would let Him, He would live His life through me, producing His fruit and giving His power. My job was to surrender to His control and be filled with His Spirit. As I submitted to the Spirit within me, my heart was filled with joy, and my life began to be filled with power and purpose. It was the most extraordinary season I had ever known. I was learning what it was like to let Christ have full control, to be filled with His Spirit and not myself. This understanding transformed my life.

Through the years, I have asked the Lord thousands of times to fill me with Himself, for when I sin (which I often do), it interrupts this filling, this control. God is always gracious to do what He promised, for this is His great desire. It is the key to life and power, joy and usefulness, and the enjoyment of His presence. Anything that God does with my life that is of value can only be attributed to one source: Christ in me, my hope of glory!

During those early days, I heard a poem quoted by Major Ian Thomas that captured my heart. It described what I was experiencing in that season … and my desire for every season since.

Just a Suit of Clothes

When Jesus died for me on Calvary,
He paid the penalty for all my sin.
He suffered all the pain my sinful heart to gain,
And now His Spirit witnesses within.

I'm just a suit of clothes that Jesus wears.
My body is the house in which He lives.
My mouth is His to talk; my feet are His to walk.

I'm just a suit of clothes that Jesus wears.

He rose again to bring abundant grace;
To justify before the Father's face.
I live no more, but He lives out His life through me.
I'm just a vessel fashioned by His grace.

As life goes on, I care not come what may.
He carries all my burdens and my cares.
For me, the battles done,
For He's the victory won!
I'm just a suit of clothes that Jesus wears.[20]

DAILY STUDY

PLANT A SEED

Read your verse and ask God to give you an opportunity to share it with someone today and explain what it means to you and can mean to them.

Ephesians 5:18 | And do not get drunk with wine, for that is dissipation, but be filled with the Holy Spirit.

DIG DEEPER

Write a paragraph about what your experience with the Spirit has been.

[20] Author Unknown, "Just a Suit of Clothes,"

Write a paragraph describing what you long for your experience to be with the Holy Spirit in the days ahead.

WRAP IT UP

Summarize what God seems to be saying to you today. What is your one-sentence takeaway?

TALK TO HIM

Spend time in prayer. Pray specifically about what you learned today.

GROUP DISCUSSION

GETTING STARTED

This week is one of the most important weeks of our study of the Presence-centered life. To walk in His presence, we must learn how to be filled (controlled) by the Holy Spirit every day and all day.

Many people don't talk about the work of the Holy Spirit. Why do you think this is true?

WATCH

As you're watching the video, write any thoughts that strike you for discussion with the group afterward.

DISCUSS

Don't feel like you have to get to every question. Let the Lord guide your conversation.

What did you learn this week about the indwelling and filling of the Holy Spirit?

Read Acts 2:41-47 aloud. List all the things that happened in the first church when they were all filled with the Holy Spirit.

What would change in your life, family, and church, if each believer was living in the fullness of the Holy Spirit?

React to this definition of the filling of the Holy Spirit. What do you think this means? Share with each other about this wonderful reality until you all understand how to be filled daily, hourly with Him.

> *The filling of the Holy Spirit is the believer's conscious, continual choice to yield control to the Holy Spirit who lives within them.*

Read aloud Galatians 5:22-23. As you realize that these are all fruits that result from being continually in God's presence and filled with His Spirit, which of these do you most long for?

PRAY

Spend some time praying these truths in as a group. (Remind the group to do their daily study for next week.)

WEEK 9

FOLLOW

DAY 1:
CHRIST EVERYWHERE

MY WIFE, HOLLY, has keen discernment, and her heart is almost always focused on the needs of others around her. One day, she was in line at the grocery store. There was no one behind her as she approached the register. She immediately noticed the distressed look on the cashier's face.

"Are you okay? Is there anything I can pray with you about?" Holly asked.

The woman began to weep and explained that her daughter had delivered a child out of wedlock, and the baby had been filled with inoperable, cancerous tumors. Holly ministered to her, prayed with her, and got her contact information. A divine moment right at the register.

Later, Holly called her, and with a growing group of other women, they began to minister to this grandmother, her daughter, and the child who was in the Children's Hospital. Soon our whole church was involved in helping this needy family.

The baby passed away after a few months. But before the child's death, we were able to see a precious string of miracles with eternal results. The grandmother returned to Christ, her daughter was saved, and the biological father of the child was also saved. The respiratory therapist who worked with the child asked us, "Who are you people and could I have a relationship with Christ too?" We also led him to Christ!

Why did all this happen? One woman simply followed God.

The "More" of Biblical Christianity

Most followers of Christ have settled for the baseline of the Christian life. They want their sins forgiven, heaven secured, and some measure of happiness in life. But there is so much more. They could be enjoying the presence of God every day as they draw near, commune with Him, and are filled with His Spirit. But even this is not the end. In fact, it is just the beginning.

Remember: you were made like God is so you could join Him in what He does. His work is to bring in His kingdom and bring people into His kingdom. You are His ambassador, now filled with His indwelling Spirit as you move through your part of the world, touching the lives of needy people.

Studies show that most of us will interact with approximately 80,000 people in our lifetime. All around us are those in whom He is working as He calls them to Himself, just like He called us. He longs for each of them to be in His presence. He wants to return them to the Garden and an eternity with Him. Sadly, we pass by them every day and are often unaware that we are God's appointed instruments to help bring them home. They're placed in our paths on purpose.

DAILY STUDY

PLANT A SEED

Read and begin to memorize …

Matthew 9:9 | "Follow Me!" and he got up and followed him.

DIG DEEPER

Do you think of your Christian walk primarily as following God, wherever He leads? Why or why not?

Has your Christian experience shown you that there are some places where you don't follow well? Where you are often unwilling to go? What steps do you struggle with?

Is your spiritual life mainly consumed with what is *inward* (for and about you) or *outward* (for and about others)? Where are you on this line? (place a mark)

1	**2**	**3**	**4**	**5**	**6**	**7**	**8**	**9**	**10**
My spiritual walk is mostly about me						My walk is mainly about others			

In his booklet *The Freedom of Self-forgetfulness,* Tim Keller wrote:

> The thing we would remember from meeting a truly gospel-humble person is how much they seemed to be totally interested in us. Because the essence of gospel-humility is not thinking more of myself or thinking less of myself, it is thinking of myself less. Gospel-humility is not needing to think about myself. Not needing to connect things with myself. It is an end to thoughts such as, "I'm in this room with these people, does that make me look good? Do I want

> to be here?" True gospel-humility means I stop connecting every experience, every conversation, with myself. In fact, I stop thinking about myself. The freedom of self-forgetfulness. The blessed rest that only self-forgetfulness brings.[1]

Read that over a few times and underline all that touches you. Then, turn those thoughts into a prayer … that God would give you a self-forgetful, and a God-and-others focused life.

WRAP IT UP

Summarize what God seems to be saying to you today. What is your one-sentence takeaway?

TALK TO HIM

Spend time in prayer. Pray specifically about what you learned today.

---

[1] Timothy Keller, *The Freedom of Self Forgetfulness*, 10Publishing, Chorely, England, 2012

DAY 2:
AN UNUSUAL APPOINTMENT

Philip was a follower of Christ and a leader in the early church. As the church began to grow, persecution arose. Acts 8 tells us that people were scattered to many places. Philip went to Samaria, which was unusual, for no one liked the Samaritans. But as he preached the gospel, a great movement occurred, and many were saved. Then, Philip received a new assignment.

> But an angel of the Lord spoke to Philip saying, "Get up and go south to the road that descends from Jerusalem to Gaza." (This is a desert road.) So he got up and went.[2]

As he traveled along this barren road, Philip saw a man in a chariot who was an official in the court of the Queen of Ethiopia returning from Jerusalem. God instructed His listening servant, "Go up and join this chariot." [3]

Philip knew how to follow God and didn't hesitate. He could have said, *Lord, this man will think I'm crazy … He doesn't want to talk with me … I won't know what to say to him … I don't have his permission to get up in his chariot … What if he rejects me? … I have a busy schedule … What if I can't speak his language?*

But this Presence-centered man didn't see objections but opportunities. He followed the promptings of the Spirit and ran ahead to the chariot. He joined God in His work. To his amazement, the man was reading the scroll of Isaiah right at the passage that spoke of Christ's sacrifice for us in what we now know as Isaiah 53. Philip began at this point and "preached Jesus" to him, which was the good news he desperately needed to hear. The man became a follower of Christ, was baptized as they came to some water, and then Philip was led away. But through Phillips's instant obedience and God's amazing grace, a man was brought into the kingdom, and the gospel spread to Africa!

Why did all this happen? One man followed God.

Both Holly and Philip (two thousand years apart) exhibited the beautiful simplicity of a Presence-centered life. We see this simplicity in a nine-word exchange between Jesus and a needy man named Matthew. It's not complicated: "Follow Me!" and he got up and followed Him.[4]

Experiencing God

"Watch to see where God is moving and join Him" is a phrase that Henry Blackaby

---

[2] Acts 8:26–27

[3] Acts 8:29

[4] Matthew 9:9

and Claude King coined in their monumental work, *Experiencing God* years ago. That thought has helped millions of people understand that God is working around us all the time. Our task is simply to join Him in His activity. We must follow without hesitation or argument. Sometimes, this calls for major adjustments in our lives. It may be a hard step, but the command is not complicated. Just follow.

To follow God in His work means that we must understand two vital truths: God-initiation and human cooperation.

DAILY STUDY

PLANT A SEED

Read and begin to memorize …

Matthew 9:9 | "__________ Me!" and he got up and "__________ him.

DIG DEEPER

Has God ever called you into a situation where you could see that He was already at work? What evidence of His work that was already in progress did you see, and how did you join Him in what He was doing?

Write about a time when the Lord led you right into a Divine encounter with someone.

What are some of the main objections that come to your mind when you feel prompted by the Holy Spirit to engage in a spiritual conversation or action with others?

Ask God for some "Divine appointments" this week (even today) and that He would give you the courage to simply and immediately follow.

WRAP IT UP

Summarize what God seems to be saying to you today. What is your one-sentence takeaway?

TALK TO HIM

Spend time in prayer. Pray specifically about what you learned today.

DAY 3:
GOD-INITIATION

One of my mentors, Manley Beasley, leaned across a table and said something to me that changed the course of my life. "Bill," he said, "the mark of a godly man is that everything he does is God-initiated."

I nodded my head as if I understood and went home thinking about this profound statement. The next day my Bible reading was in the Gospel of John. From John 5 to John 16, Jesus illustrated this truth no less than five times as He explained His life. In fact, in the New American Standard Bible, the word Christ used is translated "initiative" over and over again.

- "I can do nothing on my own initiative."[5]
- "I do nothing on my own initiative."[6]
- "I have not even come on My own initiative."[7]
- "For I did not speak on My own initiative."[8]
- "I do not speak on my own initiative, but the Father abiding in Me does His works."[9]
- "He will not speak on His own initiative, but whatever He hears, He will speak." *(Jesus speaking of the Holy Spirit when He comes.)*[10]

Many people, even believers, live their lives by nothing more than human initiation. They simply do what they decide to do. But a Presence-centered person lives like Christ did when He was on earth. Christ stayed in unceasing communion with the Father and always did what God was initiating. He always followed.

It's impossible to live by God-initiation if we have not embraced the "ways" of a Presence-centered life. We must be drawing near, communing, repenting as needed, and choosing to be filled with His Spirit to be in a posture to join Him. If these are the normal practices of our lives, and we understand the glorious calling we have to follow God in His work, we will see people and their needs. We will hear the prompting of God's Spirit and realize that we have all we need to help anyone, for God's Spirit is in us. Joining Him will be no problem.

But if we are distracted, not communing, not repenting, and not filled, we

---

[5] John 5:30

[6] John 8:28

[7] John 8:42

[8] John 12:49

[9] John 14:10

[10] John 16:13

can spend a lifetime missing the activity of God. We will walk right past our calling and destiny, and those around us will not gain the benefit of God's work through us. Life will be boring and wearisome, and we will increasingly look to other idols to fill the void.

A Presence-centered man or woman learns to live by God-initiation and is excited about the adventure. Remember our foundational statement: God's presence is our greatest need and our presence is His great desire! That's His passion for *every* man or woman, boy or girl He brings across our paths … for our colleague at work, neighbor down the street, friends and relatives, and the lady behind the counter at the grocery store. He longs to do for them what He's done for us, and we get to join Him in His eternal work! What could be more fulfilling?

DAILY STUDY

PLANT A SEED

Read and begin to memorize …

Matthew 9:9 | "Follow Me!" and he _______ ______ and followed him.

DIG DEEPER

What do you think it means, day by day, to simply follow Christ?

Describe the difference between living with human initiation and God-initiation.

Describe some of the encounters Jesus was led into as He followed God's initiation. Be specific.

Was Christ always successful in what He did as He followed the Father aggressively? Explain your answer.

In a sentence, how do you think Jesus would describe success?

WRAP IT UP

Summarize what God seems to be saying to you today. What is your one-sentence takeaway?

TALK TO HIM

Spend time in prayer. Pray specifically about what you learned today.

DAY 4:

YOUR COOPERATION

Having one ear tuned to heaven and the other tuned to the needs of those around us, we must listen to the Spirit and cooperate. My father would often speak of living a life of "aggressive cooperation" with God. If we do, we will fulfill our destiny as we join God in what He's doing. We will give godly leadership and rule in this world over the sphere that He has entrusted to us. We will be used by God to help God's kingdom come on earth as it is being done in heaven.

If you have experienced joining Him in ministry to others, you will sometimes hear what God was doing on "the other side of the story.".

My brother was leading a youth group on a mission trip. They were crossing the border into Mexico from Texas, and there was a long line of waiting trucks. His students had been trained in how to lead people to Christ, and so he encouraged them to get out of the bus and go to each truck to try to share the gospel with the truckers.

At one point, he looked down the row and saw a trucker on his knees on the pavement, and right beside him was one of his teenagers. She had nervously knocked on his truck door and asked if she could share something with him. The trucker reached toward his windshield and pulled out a worn gospel tract.

"Is it about this?" he asked. "If it is, I wish you would share with me because someone gave this little booklet to me in Dallas weeks ago, and I've read it over and over again, but I don't know what to do next!" The young girl joined in on what God had been doing for weeks in this man's life and helped bring him to Christ.

We shouldn't be surprised. God is working all the time in the people that He created and loves. We have already seen that He is relentless in His pursuit of us and longs to bring us back into His presence. But He needs His Body—the church, filled with His Spirit—to be the hands, feet, and mouths to do His work with those He's pursuing.

To never learn to follow is to miss the fullness of a Presence-centered life.

The Pleasure of the Father

I had a massive job to do years ago. I had unloaded a truckload of mulch to cover a large area in my yard. At my insistence, my two pre-teen boys were grudgingly enlisted. They weren't really willing participants, but they slowly pitched in.

My son Daniel, who was about six years old, also came out to help. His older brothers laughed at him, thinking he would be of little use. But Daniel jumped in with a vengeance. In fact, for the next few hours, he would actually fill two wheelbarrows in the time it took them to fill one. I kept spurring him on because I knew this would be a mighty lesson for him and for all of us.

The pile of mulch got smaller and finally came to an end, and we looked at the beauty of what we'd done. We were all gratified. But none of my boys were happier than Daniel.

But there was one who was filled with a greater, knowing joy—their father. I was overwhelmed with tired delight, for I had worked in the presence of my sons. It gave me pleasure to be joined by them.

God is waiting for you to join Him in His presence and *to follow Him in His work.*

DAILY STUDY

PLANT A SEED

Read and turn it into a prayer today.

Matthew 9:9 | "Follow Me!" and he got up and followed him.

DIG DEEPER

Describe a time when you followed God in ministering to someone and you discovered He'd been working in their lives all along.

Do you get bored with your life at times? Why do you think this happens?

What do you think could remedy this "spiritual boredom?" (List as many things as come to mind)

Check all of the following that apply to you.

- ☐ I'm constantly in prayer and alert to God's initiation.
- ☐ I'm often not in prayer and attuned to the Spirit's initiation.
- ☐ I think I probably miss a lot of Divine encounters.
- ☐ I spend most of my life locked into a routine that doesn't involve an awareness of God's presence.
- ☐ Even when I know the Spirit is prompting me to engage someone, for some reason, I often don't follow.
- ☐ I long to be hearing from God more through His Word and Spirit.
- ☐ I want to live like Paul and rarely miss any of God's leadership. I really want to follow well, by His grace.

In what ways is God currently using you to accomplish His will? What desires has He given you for how you can serve the kingdom going forward?

WRAP IT UP

Summarize what God seems to be saying to you today. What is your one-sentence takeaway?

TALK TO HIM

Spend time in prayer. Pray specifically about what you learned today.

DAY 5:

MY ASSIGNMENTS

God has given us all more assignments than we realize. People are all around us, and the greatest need in their lives is to experience the presence of God. Think of specific people right now that are in your life—family, neighbors, work colleagues, friends, and even enemies. Envision how their lives would dramatically change if they began to experience the nearness of God that God has planned for them.

What (or who) could possibly be used to help them see what God's presence is like? Who could be used to help create a hunger in their heart for more of Him? No one else can do that better than you, filled with God! And God has placed them right in your sphere of influence for that purpose. This is a part of the world that God created you (in His image) to rule over—not in the domineering sense, but as a place and with people that you could shepherd and lead and tend to by His leadership and grace.

For some, your encounter with them may happen in a passing moment—a waiter or waitress, a service person who comes to your home, someone seated by you on a plane. For others, you have the ability for a lifelong influence. Some need a long conversation of discipleship, others a short word of the gospel. But they all need an encounter with someone filled with God's presence.

Learning from the Best

The Apostle Paul was a master at following Jesus and bringing His presence into the lives of others. He did this everywhere he was. A Philippian jailer encountered God's presence through Paul as did the "whole Praetorian guard" in Rome (5,000 men!)[11] A small group of ladies who were by a lake were converted through God's presence as it flowed through Paul and countless others in Jewish synagogues and even on Mars Hill in Athens.[12] Paul did his job well of "ruling" over the domain that God had ordained for him and in the end could say, "I have fought the good fight, I have finished the course, I have kept the faith.[13]

This extraordinary faithfulness occurred because of Paul's God-initiated, aggressive cooperation with God every day, regardless of the cost. His life-verse could be summed up by His final words to the Ephesian leaders:

> "But I do not consider my life of any account as dear to myself, so that I may

[11] Acts 22:22-34; Philippians 1:12-14

[12] Acts 16:14; 18:4; 17:16ff

[13] 2 Timothy 4:7

finish my course and the ministry which I received from the Lord Jesus, to testify solemnly of the gospel of the grace of God. [14]

You may feel like you've not done very well at following Christ up to this point. But it is amazing how God can redeem the years if we will begin a life of following *now*. It begins by opening our hearts to the awareness of Christ's presence and our eyes to all those He's putting in our path today!

DAILY STUDY

PLANT A SEED

Read and ask God to bring someone across your path that you can share this verse with today and tell them what you're learning.

Matthew 9:9 | "Follow Me!" and he got up and followed him.

DIG DEEPER

You already have more assignments than you know. List the names of as many as you can think of whom God has placed in your sphere of influence.

Family	Friends	Colleagues	Neighbors

Acquaintances	Church friends	Enemies	Strangers

[14] Acts 20:24

List five places you frequent where Christ might want to use you to help people encounter His presence.

1.

2.

3.

4.

5.

Keep these lists and begin to pray through them daily. Ask God to let you see people with His eyes and flow through you to them with His presence. Pray they will be drawn by the presence of God in you to the God who is pursuing them. Remember, His presence is their greatest need, and their presence is His great desire.

WRAP IT UP

Summarize what God seems to be saying to you today. What is your one-sentence takeaway?

TALK TO HIM

Spend time in prayer. Pray specifically about what you learned today.

GROUP DISCUSSION

GETTING STARTED

This week describes the exciting adventure of the Presence-centered life as we follow Christ. He created us as He is so we can join Him in what He does. The Christian life is not just about knowing Christ but joining Him.

If Christ walked up to you right now (just like He did with some of His disciples) and said, "Follow Me!" what do you think He would mean?

WATCH

As you're watching the video, write any thoughts that strike you for discussion with the group afterward.

DISCUSS

Don't feel like you have to get to every question. Let the Lord guide your conversation.

Do you think of your Christian walk as primarily following God, wherever He leads? Why or why not?

Are there are some places you are unwilling to go, or where it's a struggle to go?

Share about a time when you had a "Divine encounter" with someone who needed what only Christ, through you, could give.

Share about a time when you followed God in ministering to someone and you discovered He'd been working in their lives all along.

How often do you think God wants to flow through us and touch others? What is stopping this from happening more often?

Describe the difference between living with human initiation and God-initiation.

In a sentence, how do you think Jesus would describe a successful life?

PRAY

Spend some time praying these truths in as a group. (Remind the group to do their daily study for next week.)

WEEK 10

ABIDE

DAY 1:
FINAL WORDS

A DYING MAN'S WORDS are often his most important. Final words can convey the greatest values of their lives. Often, they're reducing their life to the few things they want others to remember. Here are a few last words …

> "I go with the gladness of a boy bounding away from school. I feel so strong in Christ." (Adoniram Judson)
>
> "Live in Christ, and the flesh need not fear death." (John Knox)
>
> "If this is dying, it is the pleasantest thing imaginable." (Lady Glenorchy)
>
> "My affections are so much in heaven that I can leave you all without a regret; yet I do not love you less, but God more." (William Wilberforce)
>
> "You have been used to take notice of the sayings of dying men. This is mine: that a life spent in the service of God, and communion with Him, is the most comfortable and pleasant life that anyone can live in this world." (Matthew Henry)
>
> "Lord Jesus, I am weary in Thy work, but not of Thy work. If I have not yet finished my course, let me go and speak for Thee once more in the fields, seal the truth, and come home to die." (George Whitefield)
>
> "The best of all: God is with us!" (John Wesley)

If dying words matter so much, then we should pay great attention to the closing words of the most important Man who ever lived. As Christ was facing the final hours of His life, He gathered His disciples around him and told them what was about to happen and how they should live in the days ahead. This is recorded for us in John 14-16.

> Abide in Me, and I in you. As the branch cannot bear fruit of itself unless it abides in the vine, so neither can you unless you abide in Me. I am the vine, you are the branches; he who abides in Me and I in him, he bears much fruit, for apart from Me you can do nothing.[1]

[1] John 15:4–5

Peter, James, and John lived in a land of vineyards, so the imagery was clear and powerful to them. The vine is the source of all life and power. A branch can be cut off from the vine, yet the vine remains. But if a branch loses its connection to the vine, it will die quickly and produce no fruit.

His Sufficiency, Our Dependency

Jesus was reminding his disciples that He was the source of everything they needed. John's gospel records seven of these "I AM" statements of Christ.

"I am the bread of life." (John 6:35, our *sustenance*)
"I am the Light of the world." (John 8:12, our *illumination*)
"I am the door." (John 10:7, our *access*)
"I am the good shepherd." (John 10:11, our *protection and care*)
"I am the resurrection and the life." (John 11:25, our *eternal life*)
"I am the way and the truth and the life." (John 14:6, our *direction* and *clarity*)
"I am the true vine."[2] (John 15:1, our *source* and *power*)

Each of these metaphors is full of meaning, yet they are all simply God calling us once again and reminding us that His presence is our greatest need. He is sufficient for us in every possible way. Without Him, we have nothing that matters or lasts.

It is also a call to dependency. Just as a branch cannot survive without connecting to the vine, so we cannot survive without Christ. If we have never been connected (are not true, born-again followers of Christ), we have no life.

> He who has the Son has the life; he who does not have the Son of God does not have the life.[3]

Furthermore, the extent of our connectedness with Christ, our conscious dependency upon Him every day, will determine the measure of our fruitfulness and usefulness. If we are not drawing near and living in communion with Him, our lives will bear only the withered fruit of a self-filled life.

DAILY STUDY

Read and begin to memorize …

John 15:4-5 | Abide in Me and I in you … for apart from me you can do nothing

---

[2] John 6:35; 8:12; 10:7-11; 11:25; 14:6; 15:1-5

[3] 1 John 5:12

DIG DEEPER

Perhaps they weren't "final" words, but what are some of the most memorable words you've heard from an older believer? How did those words help you?

What do you think it means to abide in Christ?

Look at the "I am" statements listed below that Jesus used of Himself in the book of John. By each statement, write a sentence or two about what each of these mean to you, or an illustration of a time where Christ became this to you.

"I am the *bread* of life."

"I am the *Light* of the world."

"I am the *door*."

"I am the good *shepherd*."

"I am the *resurrection* and the *life*."

"I am the *way* and the *truth* and the *life*."

"I am the true *vine*."[1]

WRAP IT UP

Summarize what God seems to be saying to you today. What is your one-sentence takeaway?

TALK TO HIM

Spend time in prayer. Pray specifically about what you learned today.

[1] John 6:35; 8:12; 10:7-11; 11:25; 14:6; 15:1-5

DAY 2:
OUR ABIDING

There is one word in Jesus' discourse in John 15 that is repeated eleven times in ten verses: Jesus tells His disciples to "abide." This word means to remain in a stable or fixed condition; dwell; wait; continue.

It is possible for us to experience the nearness of God for a moment, but God desires so much more. His great pursuit, even the giving of His Son and Spirit, is not meant to give us a momentary emotional thrill or periodic spiritual high. He wants us to live with Him. To remain in His presence. To dwell there. To settle down. To make His presence our home.

He has provided all the means necessary for us to experience the joy and empowering of His continual presence, but we must choose daily to remain there.

The joy of Christianity is to learn how to remain in His presence continually. Our greatest usefulness is there. Jesus says that if we abide in Him, we will bear fruit, more fruit, much fruit, and that our fruit would remain.[2]

> Abiding leads to answered prayer. — "If you abide in Me, and My words abide in you, ask whatever you wish, and it will be done for you."[3]
>
> Abiding leads to fullness of joy. — "These things I have spoken to you so that My joy may be in you, and that your joy may be made full."[4]
>
> Abiding glorifies the Father. — "My Father is glorified by this, that you bear much fruit, and so prove to be My disciples."[5]
>
> Abiding leads to a fruitful life that fulfills our calling — "You did not choose Me but I chose you, and appointed you that you would go and bear fruit, and that your fruit would remain, so that whatever you ask of the Father in My name He may give to you."[6]

The Secret of Our Separation

We've all been pulled away. Who has not known the joy of intimacy with Him only to

---

[2] John 15:2, 4, 5, 16

[3] John 15:7

[4] John 15:11

[5] John 15:8

[6] John 15:16

look up and realize that somehow we have lost the nearness of God?

What is it that pulls us away? What do we need to know and do in order to remain in God's presence? To stay near? To experience the fullness of the Vine-life continually flowing in us and through us? One college student said, "I just don't want to lose eye-contact with Jesus!" Is that your heart's desire?

There are two primary things that keep us from abiding. And there are two things that we must consciously do to remain in His presence continually.

DAILY STUDY

PLANT A SEED

Read and begin to memorize …

John 15:4-5 | Abide in Me and I in you … for __________ from me you can do nothing.

DIG DEEPER

Read John 15:1-11. What are your observations about this beautiful teaching from Christ?

Rate these 1-10 (10 being most important) by what they mean to you personally *right now* by placing a number by each. Why do you rate them this way?

_____ Abiding leads to answered prayer. — "If you abide in Me, and My words abide in you, ask whatever you wish, and it will be done for you."

_____ Abiding leads to fullness of joy. — "These things I have spoken to you so that My joy may be in you, and that your joy may be made full."

_____ Abiding glorifies the Father. — "My Father is glorified by this, that you bear much fruit, and so prove to be My disciples."

_____ Abiding leads to a fruitful life that fulfills our calling — "You did not choose Me but I chose you, and appointed you that you would go and bear fruit, and that your fruit would remain, so that whatever you ask of the Father in My name He may give to you."

Why do you think it's so easy to be pulled away from the awareness of the presence of God?

Have you ever experienced a season of abiding in Christ, a prolonged time of sensing His presence and enjoying His being near to you? Reflect on that time and write a description of it (i.e., What started it? What did you learn? How were you changed?)

WRAP IT UP

Summarize what God seems to be saying to you today. What is your one-sentence takeaway?

TALK TO HIM

Spend time in prayer. Pray specifically about what you learned today.

DAY 3:
RESISTING DISTRACTIONS

The world is filled with distractions. Our flesh is weak, the attractions of the world are strong, and our enemy is unrelenting.

Knowing that Jesus was finally on the scene and about to begin His public ministry, what did Satan do? He came with three primary temptations to pull Christ away from His Father. Likewise, he constantly tempts us with all that is in the world.

> For all that is in the world, the lust of the flesh and the lust of the eyes and the boastful pride of life, is not from the Father, but is from the world.[7]

These distractions can be inherently sinful things or seemingly harmless things. He really doesn't care. He just doesn't want us to be consciously connected to the Vine. Paul was concerned about this.

> But I am afraid that, as the serpent deceived Eve by his craftiness, your minds will be led astray from the simplicity and purity of devotion to Christ. [8]

What if the Lord had planned a fruitful, God-glorifying evening for you to communicate with your family, think about the things of God, read the Scripture, and accomplish much in prayer, but you were diverted by a television or computer that was turned on when you came home from work and never turned off until bedtime? Your mind and attention were centered on whatever filled the screen, and you were unaware of Christ and what He desired to do. What if God planned to do significant things in those hours? Accomplish much? Help others? Bear fruit for His kingdom? But it was all lost because of a simple distraction that you didn't recognize and resist.

Distracted in Brooklyn

While I was writing this book, I had a meeting at the Brooklyn Tabernacle Church in Brooklyn, New York. It was an 8 a.m. meeting that was to be held in an ancillary building, but I was given the wrong address.

I left my hotel with plenty of time to make the meeting, and I began to walk the streets of Brooklyn. I don't know if you've ever been in downtown Brooklyn, but it was not pleasant. The streets and sidewalks were crowded, the smells were

---

[7] 1 John 2:16.

[8] 2 Corinthians 11:3

overpowering, and on top of it all, I couldn't find my building. The more I walked, the more frustrated I became.

I finally found someone who pointed me in the right direction. It was then that the Holy Spirit gently reminded me that I could have spent the last thirty minutes of walking not in frustration but in prayer.

"Oh, Father," I prayed. "I can't believe I just wasted thirty minutes that I could have spent communing with the God of the universe!" And so, I repented and began to pray.

What happened next was amazing. In five minutes of prayer, I fell in love with Brooklyn! I thought of the tremendous work Jim Cymbala and the church had done on that corner for many years, of all the glorious things that had occurred and the lives that had been changed. My heart was transformed in an instant.

Why did that occur? When you connect to the Vine, and draw near to the Father, your heart begins to beat in unison with His. You love what He loves, and you begin to join Him in His affections and, eventually, in His work.

If we want to abide in God's presence, we must recognize and resist distractions as they come. For the next few days, draw near to Christ, just as we've learned. And then ask God to make you sensitive to every distraction that pulls you away. You may discover they are the same distractions repeatedly. Resist those, firm in your faith, and choose to remain in God's presence and see what happens through an abiding life.

DAILY STUDY

PLANT A SEED

Read and begin to memorize …

John 15:4-5 | Abide in Me and I in you … for apart from me you can do __________.

DIG DEEPER

It is important to identify the particular and usual ways that the world, flesh, and devil distract you. Make a list of the 4-6 things that distract you from the presence of Christ most often. Be specific. Beside each one, prayerfully record ways that you could seek to recognize and resist these distractions.

COMMON DISTRACTIONS	HOW TO RESIST

COMMON DISTRACTIONS	HOW TO RESIST

Think back over the past 2 to 3 days. At any time, do you feel that God was calling you aside to spend time in His presence? Did you do that, or did you choose instead to do something else? What were the results?

WRAP IT UP

Summarize what God seems to be saying to you today. What is your one-sentence takeaway?

TALK TO HIM

Spend time in prayer. Pray specifically about what you learned today.

DAY 4:
EMBRACING DIFFICULTIES

Life is full of problems. Some are small and some are massive. Some are fleeting and some linger, even for a lifetime. But how we deal with the difficulties of life will determine whether we are abiding in God's presence.

Our normal path is to become upset and bothered. We get frustrated with what is happening. We may get angry at others and even at God for allowing such troubles to enter our lives. We often turn to humanistic conclusions and responses. We try our best to resolve the issues, as we lean on our own resources, disconnected from the Vine. This simply leads to greater problems.

We become frustrated, worried, bothered, and exhausted. Most tragically, we forget God and disconnect from His presence. Our lives lose His fragrance; our paths become twisted and confusing. Because we are distant from the Light, we can't see. If we lose access to the Bread of Life, we get weak and malnourished. If we miss the Truth, we are prey to the incessant lies of the Deceiver. Disconnected from the Almighty, we lose power. We begin to see the absolute truth of Christ's statement: "Apart from me, you can do nothing."[9]

So, what is the alternative? How do we abide in God's presence amid the continual difficulties of this life?

Shaking My Fist

It was the deepest hurt of my life. Years ago, something happened in my extended family that shook us to the core. (If you want to read about it and how God walked us through, read my booklet, *Forgiveness: Healing the Harbored Hurts of Your Heart*)[10] It was the most painful thing I had ever experienced. I got upset with God. *How could He let this happen*? I thought.

One night I went for a walk and stopped under a large cottonwood tree. I had prayed a sincere prayer for many years. "Lord, whatever it takes to make me a man of God, that's what I want," was my constant prayer … and I meant it. Now, I was not so sure. As I stopped under that tree, I literally shook my fist at the Father.

"God, if this is what it takes to make me a man of God, I don't think I want it," I cried.

The next few moments were some of the most sacred and important of my life. The Holy Spirit began to speak to me with clarity and grace. He reminded me that He is not the author of evil and that He was the only One who could help me through these days. He washed over my soul with unbelievable sweetness and life. He

---

[9] John 15:5

[10] Bill Elliff, *Forgiveness, Healing the Harbored Hurts of Your Heart*, https://billelliff.org/collections/all

dealt with me with perfect understanding and a precise grace.

I often say that I was holding my fists clenched saying to God, "I will not receive this into my life," which was foolish, for it was already there. There was nothing I could do about it. After the Father's gracious shepherding, I simply relaxed my hands and said, "Father, I will receive this into my life as if it were from you."

I've often said that I was accepting that circumstance and trusting that God knew what was best. As the years have passed, I have described it a bit differently: I was embracing God's sovereignty over my life. God is God and He does what He pleases, but He is good and He does what is right. Spurgeon's words (hanging now on my study wall) became real to me in that divine encounter with God's presence.

> God is too good to be unkind and too wise to be mistaken. And when we cannot trace His hand, we can always trust His Heart.

A Presence-centered life will not spare us from difficulties. We must understand that our problems are not an obstacle to God's presence but the entrance. We must let them push us to Christ, to prayer, to brokenness and dependence. Over time, we will realize that everything that touches us has come through the grid of His goodness and sovereignty. God's promises assure that He will take whatever comes and work it together for good to conform us into the image of His Son. And that transformation is worth the pressure.

DAILY STUDY

PLANT A SEED

As you've now learned this verse (and many verses) ask God to give you opportunities today to share it with others.

John 15:4-5 | Abide in Me and I in you … for apart from me you can do nothing

DIG DEEPER

What has been the toughest *obstacle* you have faced in your life? How did it affect your spiritual life?

What has been the toughest *hurt* you have faced in your life? How did it affect your daily awareness of God's presence, in either a positive or negative way?

What experience or season pulled you closer to the presence of Christ? When did you notice most greatly the nearness of God?

What is your reaction to Spurgeon's statement above? Do you believe it is true? If you have a struggle with that statement, why is it difficult for you to embrace?

Have your difficulties and hurts drawn you away from intimacy with Christ? If so, what could have been done to prevent that? How could this be different in the future?

WRAP IT UP

Summarize what God seems to be saying to you today. What is your one-sentence takeaway?

TALK TO HIM

Spend time in prayer. Pray specifically about what you learned today.

DAY 5:

BUILDING A PRESENCE-CENTERED LIFE

In the beginning of this book, we realized that God had created us in His image. He designed us so that we would be like He is and join Him in what He does. But along the way, the image has been marred, deeply affected by the influences on our lives and the choices we've made.

God has an eternal plan, though, that will not be thwarted. He wants us to experience His continual presence—our greatest need and His great desire! But we must cooperate. As we do, we begin to realize something supernatural is happening.

> Imagine yourself as a living house. God comes in to rebuild that house. At first, perhaps, you can understand what He is doing. He is getting the drains right and stopping the leaks in the roof and so on; you knew that those jobs needed doing and so you are not surprised. But presently He starts knocking the house about in a way that hurts abominably and does not seem to make any sense. What on earth is He up to? The explanation is that He is building quite a different house from the one you thought of—throwing out a new wing here, putting on an extra floor there, running up towers, making courtyards. You thought you were being made into a decent little cottage: but He is building a palace. He intends to come and live in it Himself.[11]

It is glorious, but not enough to experience God's presence for a moment. It is not enough for us, and it's not enough for our Father who longs for more. He wants us to abide with Him. And that abiding takes some testing until we learn to resist every distraction and embrace every difficulty for the glory of God.

A mature, seasoned Christian is the crown of creation. Their lives are as they should be. They still yield fruit, even in old age. They carry the image of Christ in increasing measure, and they are a testimony to all around them of what a man or woman was created to be. They are getting prepared for heaven. They are not perfect, but they have learned how to walk with God and rule well here in preparation for the work they will do for eternity.

As you look at them, do you know what has happened? They have learned how to draw near, commune, repent, be filled, follow and abide. They know now that

---

[11] C.S. Lewis, *The Weight of Glory*, Macmillan, 1980.

there is no better place to be than at home in the presence of God.

My Presence-Centered Life

In early years, I vainly thought that life was made by my own work.
I'd make my way as best I could, and so I thought
That only earthly ways would give me what was good.

The Father gently tutored me by letting go but watching still,
Until I saw my senseless pride and reached the end of my self-will.
I slowly learned that I was never meant to run alone,
but that He planned to come to me—to enter and empower me;
That mine was not a solitary race but walked in tandem step
with One whose very name is Grace.

It took some doing still. Some growing, groping, failing, learning—
Every day a mix of my distracted mind and stubborn will.
His gentle hand and voice correcting and sustaining still;
Teaching me and training me till year-by-year some ways were worked into my soul,
the steady rhythms of a Presence-centered life.

I see it now.
Still through dark glass, but brighter even as my earthly eyes grow dim.
He loves me with the fiercest love and ever calls me unto Him,
To know Him and to lean still more upon His breast.
To rest and join Him in His glorious and eternal Life.
An easy yoke.

And He will not let go.
In His Word, He's told me so, but more;
His real and present life confirms it in my heart.
His gentle voice, the kindest care. I know that He is always there.
I am His, and He is mine. It's settled now.
And so my soul abides just where it first began.
I've found my resting place.
My Presence-centered life.[12]

---

[12] My Presence-Centered Life, Bill Elliff, July 10, 2024.

DAILY STUDY

PLANT A SEED

As you've now memorized this verse and others, ask God to give you opportunities to share them with others in the coming days. Use these verses to help you enter into God's presence.

As you've seen how easy it is to memorize verses as you repeat them and meditate on them daily, why not seek to memorize a verse a week in the coming months and share them? It will help you to abide in His presence.

John 15:4-5 | Abide in Me and I in you … for apart from me you can do nothing

DIG DEEPER

Today, spend time writing a prayer to your Father. Spend time thanking Him for the specific things He's done (all the "ways" He's pursued you), and then—in detail—ask Him to help you develop all the "ways" necessary to live a Presence-centered life. Write down your heartfelt prayer to Him as a gift as you begin a new journey into His presence!

TALK TO HIM

Spend time in prayer. Pray specifically about what you learned today.

GROUP DISCUSSION

GETTING STARTED

We are finishing our final week of study of the Presence Centered Life. This is not the end, but the beginning of a life-long journey in God's presence. Let's review and talk about our foundational statement. What does this statement mean to you now?

God desires an unbroken, daily, personal relationship with us, but we must cooperate. His presence is our greatest need, and our presence is His great desire.

WATCH

As you're watching the video, write any thoughts that strike you for discussion with the group afterward.

DISCUSS

Don't feel like you have to get to every question. Let the Lord guide your conversation.

Let's remember the five ways of God in His pursuit of us: creating, calling, dwelling, indwelling, coming again. Which of these has become most impactful to you during this study? Do you feel more assured of His love and pursuit of you?

Turn to one other person in the group and share one of the main distractions that you must learn to recognize and resist to help you abide daily in God's presence. Difficulties can distract us from God's presence. Is there a difficulty, perhaps a hurt, in your past that has hindered you from drawing near to God? Share honestly about where you are in embracing God's sovereignty over your life.

What one experience or season pulled you closer to the presence of Christ?

*As you close your discussion and before you pray together, read the Epilogue out loud.

PRAY

Spend some time praying these truths in as a group. Remind the group to continue to pray for each other daily as they begin to experience the Presence Centered Life in the days ahead!

EPILOGUE

BE READY AND COME UP IN THE MORNING

Our greatest misconception is that God is uninterested in us. From the beginning, our Ancient Enemy has deceived us into thinking that God is holding out on us and that He has no interest in our fellowship. But the testimony of Scripture (and of men and women who have known Him) shatters this lie like a hammer shattering a rock.

The Divine Invitation

> "So be ready by morning, and come up in the morning to Mount Sinai, and present yourself there to Me on top of the mountain."[1]

Moses was invited by God, as a representative of the people, into His presence. He was to take no one with him—it was a solitary step. But it was to be the first business of the day to enter into the presence of the Almighty.

When Moses cooperated, "The Lord descended in the cloud and stood there with him as he called upon the name of the Lord."[2] There on that sacred spot, God revealed Himself as the "LORD, the LORD God, compassionate and gracious, slow to anger, and abounding in lovingkindness and truth, who keeps lovingkindness for thousands, who forgives iniquity, transgression, and sin."[3] Every word of that description is inviting us to meet with Him, and He will show us who He is.

So that Moses would have a full understanding, God also reminded him in this encounter that He was a God who would deal with unrepentant sin. He is gracious in His love but unwavering in His holiness.

---

[1] Exodus 34:2

[2] Exodus 34:5

[3] Exodus 34:6-7

The Natural Response

Moses did what hundreds before had done, and millions in succeeding years would imitate—he "made haste to bow low toward the earth and worship."[4] When we stand in God's holiness, we realize there is none like Him. We understand our likeness to Him but also the vast difference and that He alone deserves our unashamed worship.

Moses' prayer, in light of God's presence, was simply for more. He asked for the sustained presence of the Father. That God would accompany His people. That He would go along in their midst and not forsake them.

When you experience God's presence, you will never settle for life without Him. You realize that all you need is His nearness. "He who has God and everything else," said C.S. Lewis, "has no more than he who has God alone."[5]

The Present Call

Men and women throughout the ages have heard God's invitation. Many have failed to respond. They have not made themselves ready. They have not come up in the morning to Mount Sinai, and the results are tragic. They live lives of quiet desperation and never have the one thing that would equip them for everything. They have missed the Essential Presence.

But the way is open for every humble man and woman who will pay the price for intimacy with the One who knows them best and loves them most.

The most stunning reality is this ... *He's waiting.*

---

[4] Exodus 34:8

[5] C. S. Lewis, *The Weight of Glory*, Harper Collins, 2009, p.34.

For further study for
yourself or small groups …

THE ESSENTIAL PRESENCE

40 Days to Increased Intimacy with God

(40 daily devotionals)

THE PRESENCE CENTERED CHURCH

For more books and resources from Bill Elliff,
visit our website at **billelliff.org**

Made in the USA
Coppell, TX
22 February 2026